EAT THIS BOOK

eat
COOKING WITH
GLOBAL FRESH FLAVORS
THIS BOOK

Tyler Florence

PHOTOGRAPHS BY PETRINA TINSLAY

CLARKSON POTTER/PUBLISHERS
NEW YORK

Copyright © 2005 by Tyler Florence

Photographs copyright © 2005 by Petrina Tinslay

Published by Clarkson Potter/Publishers, New York,
New York. Member of the Crown Publishing Group,
a division of Random House, Inc.

www.crownpublishing.com
www.clarksonpotter.com

CLARKSON N. POTTER is a trademark and POTTER and
colophon are registered trademarks of Random House, Inc.

Real Kitchen is a registered trademark of
Real Kitchen Brands, LLC.

Printed in Japan

Design by Vanessa Holden

Library of Congress Cataloging-in-Publication Data
Florence, Tyler.
     Eat this book: cooking with global fresh flavors / Tyler
Florence; photographs by Petrina Tinslay. — 1st ed.
     1. Cookery.   I. Title.
     TX714.F635   2005
     641.5—dc22   2004011274

ISBN 1-4000-5237-8
10   9   8   7   6   5   4   3   2   1
First Edition

This book is dedicated to my father,
who survived cancer this year.
Dad, you're a fighter.

CONTENTS>>

PICTURE THIS ... I'm in a car on the way to a shoot for my Food Network show, *Food 911*, with David, one of my producers. I told him I was having a hard time coming up with a title for my new book. The deadline was looming and all I had were uninspired working titles.

He asked me what the cookbook was really about and I said very definitively (but not really with confidence), "It's about global fresh flavors. It's about INCREDIBLY DOABLE RECIPES that you can make at home, but it's also about global understanding through food, it's about THE FLAVORS OF DIFFERENT CULTURES. It's Tuscan farmhouse food, dishes from Chinatown, Indian curries, flavors from the Mediterranean, that you can make right here."

That same day there had been a story on the front page of the *New York Times* how the EU (European Union) was putting an import ban on American GM (genetically modified) foods like corn and wheat. Right next to that there was a story about the war in Iraq. Staring out the window, I felt that in the big picture a new cookbook was not the most important thing in the world. Yet food does transcend geographical and ideological boundaries in a way few things can.

What can I say, I'm just a chef, or maybe a frustrated politician, but I know one thing for sure: I love this country but believe we need more globalism and less globalization. I love Chinese food, Thai food, Italian, Greek, Latin American food, and French food. I love this country and I believe THROUGH FOOD THERE IS TRUE UNDERSTANDING of culture, religion, and history.

Eat This Book is a well-stamped PASSPORT OF COOKING EXPERIENCES that I've picked up from traveling, and shooting cooking shows, and over the last two years I've been practically everywhere. You can taste it throughout the book: bold Spanish flavors from Barcelona, the brilliant pan-Asian cooking styles of Australia, and the sun-kissed Mediterranean coast of France.

The chapters are all about THE ART OF LIVING AND EATING WELL, with recipes written as if you and I were having a conversation. The recipes are manageable, and after you try a few, you'll look like a superhero in the kitchen. The book speaks to everyday situations like having people over for an impromptu get-together, weekend cooking projects, and quick savory dinners. It's the kind of book that should live by the stove, dog-eared and dripped on. Whether you're hanging out at the beach or wrapped up in a thick sweater, I hope *Eat This Book* becomes A COOKING RESOURCE YOU WILL USE ALL YEAR ROUND. The recipes here are the roots of authentic cooking, not smoke and mirrors. I've been around the block a few times and I know these recipes work; they won't let you down.

But most of all, I hope you enjoy the book and this taste of the American global palate I've pulled together here. I've had the opportunity to travel, taste, and feel a lot over the last two years shooting shows for *Food 911;* my suitcase is shredded and I have seen a lot of amazing food. You don't actually have to eat this book but I do hope you tear through it with the same furious appetite that I have for life.

Tyler

EATING

THE BASICS | THE ART OF FLAVOR COMPONENTS

This first chapter offers you a new **FOUNDATION OF FLAVOR** that will make you look like a pro in the kitchen. It's full of great ideas and recipes to help you **SET UP A PANTRY** you can actually cook from. By combining a respect for the **CLASSIC** foundations like stocks and mayonnaises with **INNOVATIVE** takes on spices and herbs you get new flavor components that will turn your pantry upside down and make your cooking taste amazing. Try **QUICK THROW-TOGETHERS** like fresh-milled spices that will give a leg of lamb or even simple roast chicken unbelievable flavor; foolproof stocks for the perfect risotto; and chopped-herb sauces for everything and anything.

Herb Mayonnaises and Aïoli

I'M A MAYONNAISE JUNKIE; I KNEW THAT THE FRENCH REALLY HAD SOMETHING GOING ON WHEN I TASTED FRITES WITH AÏOLI (FRENCH FRIES WITH MAYONNAISE) FOR THE FIRST TIME AS A STUDENT TRAVELING THROUGH EUROPE. SIMPLE, CREAMY, OUTSTANDING FRESH MAYONNAISE— SINCE THEN I've been hooked. Mayonnaises and aïoli are, for the most part, the same thing. A few egg yolks, lemon juice, and good-quality oil are the foundation for both. Classic aïoli contains a fair amount of roasted garlic, which gives it a savory depth, whereas classic mayo has a bright lemony flavor. Other than that, you can go crazy with it: Lamb chops with romesco sauce, seared scallops with lemon–caper mayonnaise, and on it goes; mayo is a great flavor sidekick and really easy to make.

I usually make mayonnaise by hand. A whisk, a bowl, and that's it—nothing to clean up. But to make these variations, make the mayonnaise in the food processor to buzz it all together.

Basic Mayonnaise **Makes about 2 cups**

4 large egg yolks | 1 teaspoon dry mustard | Kosher salt and freshly ground black pepper | 1 1/2 cups canola oil | 3 tablespoons extra-virgin olive oil | 2 tablespoons fresh lemon juice

In a nonreactive bowl or in the bowl of a food processor, combine the egg yolks, mustard, and salt and pepper. Whisk or pulse in the machine just enough to break up the yolks.

If you're making this by hand, put the bowl on a damp towel to keep it from moving around. Then drizzle in the oils, whisking constantly, to form an emulsion. If the emulsion breaks (the mayonnaise will begin to look curdled and the oil will pool) don't freak—it's easy to fix. Stop drizzling and whisk until it comes together again. Then whisk in the lemon juice and 1 tablespoon of water.

If you're using the machine, pour in the oil in a thin stream, with the machine running. (The mayonnaise is unlikely to break in a processor.) Then process in the lemon juice and 1 tablespoon of water.

Taste for salt and pepper. This mayonnaise and all the variations will last for a good week, in a sealed container in the fridge.

Arugula Mayonnaise with Orange and Almond Makes about 3 cups

1 recipe Basic Mayonnaise (page 15), made in the food processor and left in the work bowl | 1 bunch of arugula, stemmed and coarsely chopped (about 1 cup chopped) | Grated zest of 1 orange | $^1/_4$ cup slivered almonds | Kosher salt and freshly ground black pepper

Take your freshly made mayonnaise, toss in the arugula, orange zest, and almonds and process to blend. Taste for salt and pepper.

Roasted Garlic Aïoli with Anchovy and Capers Makes about 2 cups

2 heads of garlic | Extra-virgin olive oil | 3 sprigs of fresh thyme | 1 recipe Basic Mayonnaise (page 15), made in the food processor and left in the work bowl | 3 anchovy fillets | 1 tablespoon capers, drained | 2 tablespoons chopped fresh flat-leaf parsley | Kosher salt and freshly ground black pepper

Preheat the oven to 400°F. Set the garlic on a square of aluminum foil and drizzle with oil. Add the thyme, fold the foil over the garlic, and seal. Roast until the garlic is tender, about 30 minutes. Squeeze the roasted garlic cloves out of their skins into the bowl of the food processor with your freshly made mayonnaise. Add the anchovies, capers, and parsley and process to combine. Taste for salt and pepper.

Mayonnaise with a Fistful of Herbs
Makes about 2 cups

$^1/_2$ cup each loosely packed fresh flat-leaf parsley, tarragon, chives, basil, mint, and cilantro leaves (about 6 tablespoons chopped) | 2 tablespoons sour cream | 1 recipe Basic Mayonnaise (page 15), made in the food processor and left in the work bowl | Kosher salt and freshly ground black pepper

Throw the herbs and sour cream into the food processor with the freshly made mayonnaise and process to blend. Taste for salt and pepper.

Curry Mayonnaise with Orange, Fresh Mint, and Peanuts Makes about 2 cups

1 teaspoon Curry Powder (page 28) | Grated zest of 1 orange | 2 tablespoons chopped fresh mint | 2 teaspoons red chile paste, such as sambal | ¼ cup chopped roasted, unsalted peanuts | 1 recipe Basic Mayonnaise (page 15), made in the food processor and left in the work bowl | Kosher salt

Add the curry powder, orange zest, mint, chile paste, and peanuts to the food processor with the freshly made mayonnaise and process to blend. Taste for salt.

Sweet Red Pepper Aïoli with Fennel and Paprika Makes about 2½ cups

Extra-virgin olive oil | 1 medium fennel bulb, trimmed and sliced (about 2 cups) | 4 garlic cloves, chopped | 1 roasted red bell pepper, stemmed, seeded, and coarsely chopped (see page 181) | 1 teaspoon sweet paprika | Pinch of saffron | 1 recipe Basic Mayonnaise (page 15), made in the food processor and left in the work bowl | Kosher salt and freshly ground black pepper

Put a sauté pan over medium-high heat and coat it with a 2-count of oil. When the oil is hot, add the fennel and the garlic and cook, stirring, until softened and lightly browned, about 10 minutes. Add the red pepper, paprika, and saffron and cook for 2 more minutes. Let that cool a little. Then dump the cooled vegetable mixture into the processor with your freshly made mayonnaise and process to blend. Taste for salt and pepper.

Lemon-Caper Mayonnaise Makes about 2 cups

Grated zest and juice of 1 lemon | **1 tablespoon capers, drained**
| **$^1/_2$ tablespoon chopped fresh flat-leaf parsley** | **1 recipe Basic Mayonnaise
(page 15), made in the food processor and left in the work bowl** |
Pinch of kosher salt

Add the lemon juice and zest, capers, and parsley to the food
processor with the mayonnaise and process to blend. Taste for salt.

Romesco Sauce Makes about 2 cups

2 garlic cloves, chopped | **1 roasted red bell pepper (see page 181),
stemmed, seeded, and torn into narrow strips** | **$^1/_2$ cup walnuts, ground in
a food processor to a coarse powder** | **1 fresh hot red chile, stemmed** |
Pinch of sugar | **Juice of $^1/_2$ lemon** | **1 recipe Basic Mayonnaise (page 15),
made in the food processor and left in the work bowl** | **Kosher salt and
freshly ground black pepper**

Add the garlic, roasted red bell pepper, ground walnuts, chile, sugar,
and lemon juice to your freshly made mayonnaise in the food processor
and process to blend. Taste for salt and pepper.

Fresh Chopped-Herb Sauces

MOST REALLY GOOD RECIPES ARE INVENTED OUT OF NECESSITY. ONE NIGHT I WAS COOKING DINNER FOR A FRIEND OF MINE. IT WAS KIND OF LATE, AND BOTH OF US HAD A REALLY BUSY DAY. SO I SEARED TWO BEAUTIFUL RUBY TUNA STEAKS AND SIMPLY CHOPPED SOME FENNEL WITH A FEW cherry tomatoes, black olives, orange zest, and a handful of fresh basil. I tossed it with olive oil and a little lemon juice and spooned it over the tuna. It tasted so clean and fresh, and the olive oil made the vegetables juicy. I jotted the idea down in my flavor journal, and when it came time to start writing recipes for the book, I wanted to see how far I could take the idea. I call it chopped-herb sauces and I use this technique all the time. You can take it to a lot of different directions—Asian, Mediterranean, southwestern—it all works. Just buzz through some ingredients like parsley, raisins, capers, and pine nuts with a cleaver and season them with olive oil, lemon juice, maybe a little red wine vinegar. A lot of the chopped-herb sauces are served with dishes in the book, such as seared scallops with a sauce of pomegranate, walnuts, and parsley (see page 226). They're rustic and incredibly tasty and look great on a plate. It's the savory equivalent of the first guy who left grapes out in the sun too long.

Parsley, Raisin, Caper, and Pine Nut Sauce Makes about 1 cup

¼ cup golden raisins, coarsely chopped | 3 tablespoons capers, drained and coarsely chopped | 3 tablespoons pine nuts, coarsely chopped | 3 anchovy fillets, finely chopped | ½ bunch of fresh flat-leaf parsley, chopped (½ cup) | ¼ cup extra-virgin olive oil | Juice of 1 lemon | Kosher salt and freshly ground black pepper

Stir up all of the ingredients together in a bowl and season with salt and pepper.

Parsley, Green Apple, and Curry Sauce
Makes about 2 cups

$^1/_2$ **bunch of fresh flat-leaf parsley, chopped ($^1/_2$ cup)** | **2 Granny Smith apples (skin on), cored and cut into small dice** | **2 tablespoons fresh thyme leaves** | **1 tablespoon Curry Powder (see page 28)** | **1 tablespoon maple syrup** | $^1/_4$ **cup extra-virgin olive oil** | **Juice of 1 lemon** | **Kosher salt and freshly ground black pepper**

Stir up all of the ingredients together in a bowl and season with salt and pepper.

Parsley, Pimiento, and Green Olive Sauce **Makes about 1 cup**

$^1/_2$ **bunch of fresh flat-leaf parsley, chopped ($^1/_2$ cup)** | **4 pimientos, chopped** | **12 pitted green olives, coarsely chopped** | **Juice of 1 lemon** | $^1/_4$ **cup extra-virgin olive oil** | **Kosher salt and freshly ground black pepper**

Stir it all up together in a bowl and season with salt and pepper.

Grapefruit, Tarragon, and Green Olive Sauce **Makes about 1 $^1/_2$ cups**

1 grapefruit | $^1/_2$ **cup pitted green olives, coarsely chopped** | **1 tablespoon chopped fresh tarragon** | **1 teaspoon crushed black peppercorns** | **2 table-spoons extra-virgin olive oil** | **1 tablespoon fresh lemon juice** | **Kosher salt**

Cut about $^1/_2$ inch off the top and bottom of the grapefruit and stand it on end. Then take a big knife and cut off all of the skin, including as much of the white pith as you can. Pick up the grapefruit and, holding it over a good-size bowl so you don't lose any of the juice, cut between the membranes with a small knife to cut out the sections. When you're finished, squeeze what's left of the grapefruit over the bowl to get as much juice as you can. Coarsely chop the grapefruit sections and swipe them into the bowl, too. Stir in the rest of the ingredients and season to taste with salt.

Cilantro, Fresh Ginger, Dried Shrimp, and Chili Sauce **Makes about ¹/₂ cup**

¹/₂ bunch of fresh flat-leaf parsley, chopped (¹/₂ cup) | ¹/₂ bunch of fresh cilantro, chopped (¹/₂ cup) | ¹/₄ cup chopped dried shrimp | 1 tablespoon grated fresh ginger | 1 tablespoon soy sauce | ¹/₄ teaspoon red chile paste, such as sambal | Pinch of sugar | ¹/₄ cup extra-virgin olive oil | 1 tablespoon fresh lemon juice | Kosher salt and freshly ground black pepper

Stir it all up together in a bowl and season with salt and pepper.

Basil, Olive, Tomato, and Fennel Sauce
Makes about 2 cups

1 bunch of fresh basil, chopped (about ¹/₂ cup) | ¹/₂ cup each of pitted black and green olives, coarsely chopped | 1 cup cherry tomatoes, crushed by hand | Grated zest of 1 orange | 1 tablespoon fennel seeds | ¹/₂ cup extra-virgin olive oil | 1 tablespoon fresh lemon juice | Kosher salt and freshly ground black pepper

Stir up all of the ingredients together in a bowl and season with salt and pepper.

Mint, Chile, Lime, and Onion Sauce
Makes about 1 cup

1 bunch of fresh mint, chopped (about ¹/₂ cup) | 1 small fresh hot green chile (I use a Thai bird chile) with seeds, chopped | Grated zest of 1 lime | Juice of 1 lime | 1 medium onion, chopped | ¹/₄ cup extra-virgin olive oil | Kosher salt and freshly ground black pepper

Stir all of the ingredients up together in a bowl and season with salt and pepper.

Pomegranate, Walnut, Celery Leaf, and Parsley Sauce **Makes about 1 cup**

**¹/₂ cup whole pomegranate seeds (from 1 small pomegranate) |
¹/₄ cup toasted walnut pieces, chopped | ¹/₄ cup celery leaves, chopped |
1 tablespoon chopped fresh flat-leaf parsley | Grated zest of 1 orange
| 3 tablespoons extra-virgin olive oil | 1 tablespoon fresh lemon juice |
Kosher salt and freshly ground black pepper**

Stir up all the ingredients together in a bowl and taste for salt and pepper.

Fig, Black Olive, Cilantro, and Lemon Sauce **Makes about 1 ¹/₂ cups**

**1 cup coarsely chopped dried Mission figs (6 to 8) | ¹/₂ cup pitted black
olives, coarsely chopped | Grated zest of 1 lemon | Juice of 1 lemon |
1 tablespoon capers, drained and coarsely chopped | 1 tablespoon chopped
fresh cilantro | 2 tablespoons extra-virgin olive oil | Kosher salt and freshly
ground black pepper**

Stir it all up together in a bowl and season to taste with salt and pepper.

Fresh-Milled Spices

ONCE A YEAR I GUT OUT MY PANTRY, REORGANIZE EVERYTHING, AND START OVER. IT GIVES ME A CHANCE TO THROW THINGS AWAY, AND THIS YEAR I ACTUALLY FOUND AN OLD CONTAINER OF GROUND CUMIN, I THINK FROM COLLEGE. THE LABEL WAS TORN AND STAINED. I TOOK ONE LOOK AT IT, GOT A LITTLE MISTY, and tossed it right in the bin and didn't look back. True story, but my point is if you have that little tube of ground pepper that you got in a picnic basket ten years ago, chuck it out. Buy whole spices and grind them yourself. Get one of those inexpensive black coffee grinders, toast the seeds, and grind them up. I promise, this one step will dramatically improve the way you cook.

You can make up your own tour of flavors or try some of the recipes I devised. When I cleaned up this year, I found a half bag of dried porcini mushrooms. I ground them with garlic powder and sea salt and rubbed the mixture onto a chicken, then roasted it. Amazing! It was one of the best things I've tasted all year.

These spice mixtures must all be cooked before eating. Sprinkle them on whatever you like and grill, sauté, or roast. (The Japanese-style Grapefruit and Nori Powder on page 29 is dynamite with scallops: Dab it on those babies and cook 'em.)

A word of advice: If you're using your coffee grinder to grind these mixtures, make sure you thoroughly wipe it out before you make coffee again; they'll make your coffee taste just awful.

North African Spice Mix Makes about ¹⁄₂ cup

2 cinnamon sticks, broken in pieces | 16 whole cloves | 4 teaspoons cumin seeds | 1 tablespoon coriander seeds | 2 teaspoons fennel seeds | 1 teaspoon whole black peppercorns | 2 tablespoons sweet paprika | 1 tablespoon kosher salt

In a dry skillet over low heat, combine the cinnamon, cloves, cumin, coriander, fennel, peppercorns, and sweet paprika and toast for about 1 minute, or until you can smell the spices (the heat releases their oils). Shake the pan while heating so that the spices don't scorch. Transfer to a spice mill or clean coffee grinder, add the salt, and grind to a powder. Use immediately or store in a sealed jar for up to 2 months.

Curry Powder Makes about ¹/₂ cup

2 tablespoons coriander seeds | 1 tablespoon cumin seeds | 1 teaspoon fennel seeds | ¹/₂ teaspoon whole cloves | ¹/₂ teaspoon mustard seeds | 1 tablespoon cardamom seeds | 1 tablespoon whole black peppercorns | 2 dried red chiles, broken in pieces, seeds discarded | 1 tablespoon ground turmeric

In a small, dry skillet, combine the coriander, cumin, fennel, cloves, mustard seeds, cardamom, peppercorns, and chiles. Toast over medium-low heat, shaking the pan often to prevent the spices from burning, for a couple of minutes until the spices smell fragrant. Let the spices cool. In a clean coffee grinder, grind the toasted spices to a fine powder. Add the turmeric and give it another quick buzz to combine. Use immediately or store in a sealed jar for up to 2 months.

Turkish Spice Mix Makes about ¹/₂ cup

3 tablespoons allspice berries | 2 teaspoons whole black peppercorns | 2 teaspoons fennel seeds | 2 teaspoons cumin seeds | 2 teaspoons coriander seeds | 1-inch piece of cinnamon stick | 1 teaspoon whole cloves

Combine the spices in a dry skillet over low heat and toast for about 1 minute, or until you can smell the spices (the heat releases their oils). Shake the pan while heating so the spices don't scorch. Let them cool. Transfer to a spice mill or clean coffee grinder and grind to a powder. Use immediately or store in a sealed jar for up to 2 months.

Ancho Chili Powder **Makes about ¾ cup**

3 ancho chiles, seeded and hand-torn into pieces | ¼ cup chili powder
| 2 tablespoons ground coriander | 1 tablespoon ground cumin |
2 teaspoons sweet paprika | 1 tablespoon dried oregano |
1 tablespoon garlic powder | ¼ teaspoon ground cinnamon

In a dry skillet, toast the ancho chile pieces over low heat until
fragrant, shaking the pan so they don't scorch. Put the chiles in a mini
food processor and pulse to a powder. Add the remaining ingredients
and buzz again to combine. Use immediately or store in a sealed jar for
up to 2 months.

Porcini Powder **Makes about ½ cup**

½ cup dried porcini mushroom pieces | 1 teaspoon onion powder
| 1 teaspoon garlic powder | 1 teaspoon kosher salt

Put everything into a spice mill or clean coffee grinder and grind to a
fine powder. Use immediately or store in a sealed jar for up to 2 months.

Grapefruit and Nori Powder **Makes about ¼ cup**

Zest of 1 grapefruit, stripped off with a Microplane and dried on a plate
overnight (see Note) | 1 nori sheet, quickly passed over a flame to toast,
broken into pieces | 1 teaspoon black sesame seeds | 1 teaspoon wasabi
powder | 1 teaspoon kosher salt

Combine the zest, nori, and sesame seeds in a spice mill and process
until finely ground. Add the wasabi and salt and process again. Use
immediately or store in a sealed jar for up to 2 months.

NOTE | If you don't have a Microplane, strip off the zest with a
vegetable peeler and bake in a low oven for about 1 hour, or until dry.

Vinaigrettes

SO WHAT'S IT GOING TO BE TONIGHT? OLIVE OIL, BALSAMIC, AND ORANGE? OR SESAME OIL, SOY SAUCE, AND LIME? SOMETIMES IT'S A TOUGH CALL, BUT THE PANTRY IS WHERE ALL THE ACTION HAPPENS IN THE KITCHEN. LET'S JUST SAY THAT YOU HAVE A BEAUTIFUL SALMON FILLET AND YOU'RE NOT SURE what to do with it. With a well-balanced vinaigrette you can really make it sing. I break the flavors up into two camps: high notes and low notes. The high notes are anything that has an acidic or a salty quality: for example, balsamic vinegar, rice wine vinegar, or soy sauce. The low notes are what make vinaigrettes taste rich—generally the oils—such as extra-virgin olive oil, sesame oil, or maybe walnut oil. Then the balance comes into play. A little mustard, or a few drops of Asian chili sauce for enough heat to warm the tongue. Finally, a little geography: fresh tarragon, and finely minced shallots or ginger, cilantro, scallions. The salmon won't know what hit it.

Classic French Vinaigrette Makes about 1 1/2 cups

1 teaspoon Dijon mustard | **1/4 teaspoon kosher salt** | **Pinch of sugar** | **1 tablespoon fresh lemon juice** | **1 tablespoon white wine vinegar** | **1 tablespoon finely chopped shallot** | **1/2 cup grapeseed oil, or other light-flavored oil** | **1/4 cup extra-virgin olive oil** | **Freshly ground black pepper**

Put all of the ingredients into a jar, screw on the lid, and shake it all up to emulsify. Taste for salt and pepper.

VARIATIONS | Add 1 to 2 tablespoons finely chopped fresh herbs such as flat-leaf parsley, chives, chervil, and dill; add 1 teaspoon minced garlic; add 1 tablespoon grated daikon radish; replace the vinegar with an equal amount of red wine, sherry wine, or rice wine vinegar; replace the olive oil with another flavorful oil such as hazelnut or walnut.

Citrus-Chile Vinaigrette **Makes about ³⁄₄ cup**

1 vine-ripe tomato, seeded and chopped | 2 canned chipotle peppers in adobo, chopped | 1 teaspoon sugar | Juice and zest of 1 orange | Juice and zest of 1 lime | Juice and zest of 1 lemon | ¹⁄₄ cup extra-virgin olive oil | Kosher salt and freshly ground black pepper

In a blender, purée the tomato, chipotles, sugar, citrus juices, and zests until smooth. Pour in the olive oil and purée again until emulsified and slightly thickened. Season to taste with salt and pepper.

Ginger-Soy Vinaigrette **Makes about 1 cup**

4 big handfuls of fresh cilantro, finely chopped | 1 jalapeño, sliced | 1 teaspoon minced fresh ginger | 1 garlic clove, minced | Juice of 4 limes | ¹⁄₄ cup low-sodium soy sauce | ¹⁄₄ teaspoon sugar | ¹⁄₄ cup extra-virgin olive oil | Kosher salt and freshly ground black pepper

In a mixing bowl, combine the cilantro, jalapeño, ginger, garlic, lime juice, soy sauce, sugar, oil, and salt and pepper to taste. Stir the ingredients together until it's all well blended.

Sweet Chili Sauce with Lime **Makes about ³⁄₄ cup**

6 tablespoons honey | 3 tablespoons red chile paste, such as sambal | 2 tablespoons rice vinegar | 1 tablespoon low-sodium soy sauce | Juice of ¹⁄₂ lime | 1 garlic clove, minced | 1 teaspoon minced fresh ginger

Put all of the ingredients into a small bowl and stir to combine.

Stocks

I WAS IN ALBA, THIS BEAUTIFUL AREA IN PIEMONTE, ITALY, WITH THIS COUPLE—SHE DID THE COOKING AT THE BED-AND-BREAKFAST WHERE I WAS STAYING. HE, AMONG MANY THINGS, WAS A TRUFFLE HUNTER, A THREE-TIME WORLD-CHAMPION TRUFFLE HUNTER. SHE MADE A CLASSIC RISOTTO with the most beautiful chicken stock, one of the best I've tasted. It was rich and golden and had only enough vegetables to give the chicken flavor. She explained to me that a risotto is only as good as the *brodo,* or broth, that you use. She ladled the golden stock into the big pot of rice and stirred, as the natural starch became creamy silk. The risotto tasted rich and nourishing, like savory melted ice cream. Then Ezzo, the hunter husband, walked in behind her, pulled out a golden white truffle from a cloth in his pocket, and shaved half of it into the rice. The truffles tasted like sex; the humble risotto with the rich chicken stock tasted like heaven.

Fish Stock 45 minutes | Makes 2 quarts

3 pounds fish bones from non-oily fish such as flounder or cod, well rinsed so that there is absolutely no blood on the bones | 1 onion, cut in half | 1 leek, cut into large pieces | 3 celery stalks, cut into large pieces | 1 small fresh chile | 1 big strip of orange zest | 1 big strip of lemon zest | 4 bay leaves | 1 bunch of fresh thyme | 1 teaspoon whole black peppercorns | 1/2 cup white wine

Combine all of the ingredients in a large stockpot. Pour in only enough cold water to cover (about 2¼ quarts). Bring to a boil over medium heat. Reduce the heat and simmer gently for 20 minutes. As the stock cooks, skim any foam and impurities that rise to the surface; add a little more water if necessary to keep the bones covered while cooking.

Strain the stock through a fine-mesh sieve into another pot to remove the bones and vegetable solids; discard them. Use the stock immediately or, if you plan on storing it, place the pot in a sink full of ice water and stir to cool down the stock. When cool, transfer to a storage container, cover, and refrigerate for a day or two, or freeze.

Clam Broth with Bacon and Fresh Thyme

30 minutes | **Makes about 1 quart**

4 slices bacon (preferably double-smoked), chopped | **2 garlic cloves, minced** | **Juice of $1/2$ lemon** | **1 dozen quahog or chowder clams, scrubbed and soaked to remove dirt** | **$1/2$ cup white wine**

Put a large pot over medium heat, add the bacon, and sauté until the fat is rendered and the bacon is browned, about 5 minutes. Remove the cooked pieces from the pot and drain, then reserve for another use. Add the garlic and lemon juice to the bacon drippings and cook, stirring, for 2 to 3 minutes. Add the clams, white wine, and $2^{1}/_{2}$ cups of water and bring to a low boil. Reduce the heat, cover the pot, and simmer for 10 or 15 minutes to steam open the clams. Remove the clams from the pot, discarding any that don't open. Strain the broth into a bowl. Pull the clams out of their shells, chop them, and add to the bowl with the broth. (Discard the shells.) Use the broth immediately or, if you plan on storing it, put the bowl in a sink full of ice water and stir to cool down the broth. Transfer to a storage container and refrigerate for a day or two, or freeze.

Rich Chicken Stock $1^{1}/_{2}$ hours | Makes 2 quarts

1 chicken (about $3^{1}/_{2}$ pounds), free range if you can get it | **1 rutabaga, cut in large chunks** | **2 carrots, cut in large chunks** | **2 celery stalks, cut in large chunks** | **2 large onions, quartered** | **1 turnip, halved** | **1 head of garlic, halved** | **$1/4$ bunch of fresh thyme** | **2 bay leaves** | **1 teaspoon whole black peppercorns**

Remove the giblets from the chicken. Discard the liver (it makes the stock bitter) and hold on to everything else. Rinse the chicken with cool water. Put the chicken, vegetables, and giblets in a large stockpot. Pour in enough cold water to cover by 1 inch (about 3 quarts); too much will make the broth taste weak. Toss in the herbs and peppercorns and allow the stock to slowly come to a boil over medium heat. Skim off the foam, then reduce the heat and simmer gently for 1 hour, uncovered, until the chicken is cooked through. As the stock cooks, skim any impurities that rise to the surface; add a little more water if necessary to keep the chicken covered while simmering.

Carefully remove the chicken to a cutting board. When it is cool enough to handle, discard the skin and bones; shred the meat by hand into a storage container and reserve for soups or salads.

In the meantime, set a large, fine-mesh sieve or a large strainer lined with cheesecloth (the cheesecloth will remove some of the excess fat) over another pot. Pour the stock into the sieve or strainer to strain out the vegetable solids; discard. Use the stock immediately or, if you plan on storing it, place the pot in a sink full of ice water and stir to cool down the stock. Transfer to a storage container, cover, and refrigerate for up to 1 week, or freeze.

Chinese Chicken Stock 1 1/2 hours | Makes 2 quarts

1 chicken (3 1/2 to 4 pounds), free range if you can get it | 1 yellow onion, halved | 1 bunch of green onions, trimmed and halved | 4 garlic cloves, smashed | 3-inch piece of fresh ginger, whacked open with the flat side of a knife | 1 teaspoon whole white peppercorns

Remove the giblets from the chicken and reserve everything but the liver (it makes the stock bitter). Rinse the chicken with cool water. Put the chicken and giblets in a large stockpot. Toss in the yellow onion, green onions, garlic, ginger, and peppercorns. Pour about 3 quarts of cold water into the pot to cover the chicken by 1 inch and bring it to a simmer over medium heat. Skim off the foam, reduce the heat, and simmer gently, uncovered, for 1 hour, or until the chicken is cooked through. Skim off the foam that rises to the surface periodically. Add a little more water if necessary to keep the chicken covered while simmering.

Carefully remove the chicken from the pot and let it cool. Pull the meat off the bones. Remove the skin and shred the meat by hand into a storage container; reserve for soups and salads.

In the meantime, set a large, fine-mesh sieve or a large strainer lined with cheesecloth (the cheesecloth will remove some of the excess fat) over another pot. Pour the stock into the sieve or strainer to strain out the vegetable solids; discard. Use the stock immediately or if you plan on storing it, put the pot in a sink full of ice water and chill it down, stirring every now and then. Transfer to a storage container, cover, and refrigerate for up to 1 week, or freeze.

Roasted Veal Stock with Red Wine

1 hour + simmering time | Makes 2 quarts

5 pounds veal knuckle bones, rinsed well and drained | 2 tablespoons extra-virgin olive oil | Kosher salt and freshly ground black pepper | $^1/_4$ cup tomato paste | 4 carrots, cut in half | 2 celery stalks, cut in half | 2 onions, cut in half | 1 head of garlic, halved horizontally | $^1/_2$ bottle red wine | $^1/_2$ bunch of fresh thyme | 2 bay leaves | 1 teaspoon whole black peppercorns

Preheat the oven to 450°F.

Put the veal bones in a roasting pan, drizzle with the olive oil, and sprinkle with salt and pepper. Put them in the oven and roast until good and browned all over, about 30 minutes. Then remove the pan from the oven and paint the bones with the tomato paste. Put the pan back into the oven and roast for another 20 minutes.

Transfer the bones to a large stockpot. Add all of the vegetables and the wine. Pour in only enough cold water to cover the bones (more will make the stock weak). Toss in the herbs and peppercorns and bring the stock slowly to a boil over medium heat. Reduce the heat and simmer gently, uncovered, for 3 to 4 hours. As the stock cooks, skim any foam and impurities that rise to the surface; add a little more water if necessary to keep the bones covered while simmering.

Strain the stock through a fine-mesh sieve into another pot to remove the bones and vegetable solids; discard. Use the stock immediately or, if you plan on storing it, set the pot in a sink full of ice water and stir to cool down the stock. When cool, transfer to storage containers, cover, and refrigerate for up to 1 week, or freeze.

DEVOURING

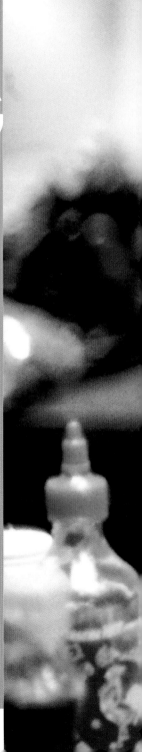

This chapter is an updated collection of recipes that yield **LITTLE BITES OF FOOD** that your guests will devour. The recipes are super easy to follow. Pull them out for cocktail parties. **PASS THEM AROUND** as a light dinner, or snack on them when you're lying around watching movies.The fingerling potatoes with crème fraîche and caviar work great as a passed hors d'oeuvre, the fried zucchini blossoms with fresh lemon and sea salt are **SHOW STOPPING**. The field mushrooms roasted with sausage, raisins, and olives are fantastic as a starter to a main course.

DEVOURING

Blue Cheese Crostini with Sancerre Syrup and Peppery Lettuce

30 minutes | Serves 4

I have a well-loved pizza stone in my oven that I tend to use much more for making the croutons in this recipe than I actually do for pizza. I like the Sancerre syrup quite a bit; its flavor is beautifully salty-sweet with the melted blue cheese. Everybody loves this. It's like a crunchy cheese course.

Preheat the oven to 500° F. Put a sheet pan or pizza stone in the oven so that it gets good and hot.

In a saucepan, combine the wine, honey, and lemon juice and heat over medium-low. Simmer gently, swirling the pot every now and then for even cooking, for 15 to 20 minutes, until the wine is syrupy and thick enough to coat the back of a spoon.

Butter both sides of the baguette slices. Put a good hunk of cheese on top of each slice. When your sauce is ready, put the crostini on the hot sheet pan or pizza stone and bake for 5 minutes, until the cheese melts and the bread is nicely toasted.

Put the lettuce in a mixing bowl and toss with the olive oil, salt, and pepper. Divide the greens among 4 serving plates and put 3 crostini on the side of each plate. Drizzle the wine syrup over the crostini and greens, and sprinkle with the walnuts.

1 $^1/_2$ cups dry white wine, such as Sancerre or Sauvignon Blanc

$^1/_4$ cup orange blossom honey

Juice of $^1/_2$ lemon

3 tablespoons unsalted butter

$^1/_2$ baguette, cut into 1-inch slices (12 slices)

8 ounces excellent-quality blue cheese

1 bunch of peppery lettuce, such as arugula or watercress

2 tablespoons extra-virgin olive oil

Kosher salt and freshly ground black pepper

$^1/_4$ cup toasted chopped walnuts

Toasted Almonds in Chile Oil

20 minutes | Makes 1 ¼ cups

I adapted this recipe from one of my favorite restaurants in the country. Every time you sit down in the beautiful dining room at Luques in Los Angeles, Susanne sends out amazing small bowls of almonds that are juicy with olive oil and spiked with a few snowflakes of sea salt. Here is my take on it.

½ cup extra-virgin olive oil

1 fresh hot red chile, split

½ pound whole raw almonds, not skinned

½ teaspoon kosher salt

Preheat the oven to 375°F.

Heat the oil in a large ovenproof skillet over medium heat for a couple of minutes to get it nice and hot. Add the chile and cook for about 1 minute to let it infuse the oil with its flavor. Add the almonds and cook, stirring, to coat them completely with the chile oil, about 2 minutes. Now put the whole pan in the oven and roast for 15 minutes, or until the nuts are toasty and fragrant. Remove to a plate lined with paper towels and sprinkle with the salt while they're still hot.

Fried Zucchini Blossoms

30 minutes | Makes 12 blossoms

The blossoms are a fantastic treat in the summer, but if they're out of season the batter works great as a Japanese tempura for vegetables such as green beans or asparagus.

Peanut oil, for deep-frying

1 large egg yolk

1 cup ice water

1 cup all-purpose flour

12 zucchini blossoms

Kosher salt and freshly ground black pepper

Pour 2 to 3 inches of oil into a deep-fat fryer, wok, or deep, heavy pot and heat to 375°F. on a frying thermometer.

In a large mixing bowl, lightly beat the egg yolk with a fork until smooth and then pour in the ice water. Stir to combine. Slowly add the flour and continue to mix with the fork until the batter is the consistency of heavy cream.

When your oil is up to temperature, take a blossom in each hand, holding them by the ends of the stems. Dip each into the batter to coat completely. Let the excess drip off. Then gently slide the blossoms into the hot oil and fry for 2 minutes, or until the blossoms are crisp and golden brown. Drain on paper towels. Go ahead and cook all the rest the same way. Season with salt and pepper while the blossoms are still hot and serve immediately.

Grilled Fig Toasts with Prosciutto and Green Beans

45 minutes | Serves 6

This salad is beautiful in the summertime. The ripe figs and the prosciutto taste amazing with the honey-butter vinaigrette.

Bring a large pot of salted water to a boil. Fill a large bowl with ice water and add salt to it until it tastes slightly salty. You're going to refresh the cooked beans in this water bath and you want salt in there so that the ice water doesn't leach out the salt absorbed by the beans during cooking. When the water comes to a boil, add the beans and cook until just tender, about 3 minutes. Drain, then refresh in the water bath to keep the bright green color, and drain well again. Put the beans in a bowl with the prosciutto and basil and set that aside.

Whip the softened butter and honey together.

Put a large grill pan on two burners over medium-high heat or pre-heat an outdoor gas or charcoal barbecue and get it very hot. Take a few paper towels and fold them several times to make a thick square. Blot a small amount of oil on the paper towels, then carefully and quickly wipe the hot grates of the grill to make a nonstick grilling surface. Cut the figs in half, brush with olive oil, and grill, cut sides down, until heated through, about 3 minutes. Remove to a platter.

Now put the bread slices on the grill and grill on both sides until marked and crisp, 3 to 4 minutes total. Brush one side of each slice with the honey butter (you'll have some of the honey butter left over; you'll need it for the vinaigrette). Put a slice of toast in the center of each of 6 serving plates, buttered side up. Arrange 4 to 5 fig halves on top of each. Melt the remaining honey butter in a small sauté pan over medium heat and cook until it begins to brown. Add the shallot and cook for 1 minute. Stir in the vinegar and olive oil and pour the dressing over the beans. Toss and season with salt and pepper. Mound the bean salad on top of each toast and serve.

Kosher salt
1 pound green beans, trimmed
2 ounces thin-sliced prosciutto, torn into pieces ($1/2$ cup)
Small handful of fresh basil leaves, shredded by hand
$1/2$ cup (1 stick) unsalted butter, at room temperature
$1/4$ cup honey
$1/2$ cup extra-virgin olive oil, plus extra for brushing the grill and the figs
1 pint fresh Black Mission figs
1 pint fresh green figs
6 slices store-bought nut bread
1 shallot, minced
3 tablespoons sherry vinegar
Freshly ground black pepper

Scallop Ceviche with Melon, Chile, and Mint

45 minutes + marinating time | Serves 6

For me, scallops are the perfect seafood. Buttery, soft, and oceany, they always show up on my menus. The scallops in this dish are marinated in citrus juices and paired up with beautiful chunks of sweet melon. Mint and the chiles throw the flavor through the roof.

1 pound very fresh shucked bay
  or sea scallops

Kosher salt and freshly ground
  black pepper

Juice and zest of 2 oranges

Juice and zest of 2 lemons

Juice and zest of 2 limes

2 teaspoons sugar, plus a pinch
  for the cantaloupe

Extra-virgin olive oil

$1/2$ small ripe cantaloupe, halved,
  seeded, peeled, and cut into
  small cubes

$1/4$ bunch of fresh mint, hand-torn

$1/2$ fresh hot red chile, cut into
  paper-thin rounds

Pull off and discard the small, tough, crescent-shaped muscle on the side of each scallop (that's the muscle that connects the scallop to its shell). Use your fingers; the muscles will come off easily. Using a sharp knife, slice the scallops horizontally into 2 discs (or 3, if the scallops are very large); the thinner they are, the faster they'll "cook." Put the scallops in a glass bowl and season with a fair amount of salt and pepper.

Put the citrus juices and zests and the 2 teaspoons of sugar in a blender and give it a whirl to combine. Add a 3-count of olive oil and blend again to emulsify. Pour the marinade over the scallops. There should be enough juice so that the scallops float freely. Cover and refrigerate for at least 2 hours, until the scallops are opaque. That means that they've been "cooked" by the acid in the fruit.

In a separate bowl, combine the cantaloupe, mint, and chile; season with a pinch of sugar and salt and pepper and toss gently to combine.

Serve the ceviche with a little bit of the citrus juice, topped with a spoonful of the cantaloupe salad.

Creamy Smoked Trout with Apple, Celery, and Crisp Brown Bread

35 minutes | Serves 6

Last Christmas, I put this dish together for a magazine article. The piece was about simple flavors for the holidays, and I think this dish really pulls it off. It's creamy, crunchy, smoky, and sweet all at once, and served on some crisp brown bread it looks and tastes like the holidays. Whenever I set out a bowl of it, it comes back practically licked clean.

Preheat the oven to 500°F.

In a large mixing bowl, toss together the flaked trout, apples, chives, and celery until well combined. In another bowl, whisk together the horseradish, sour cream, mayonnaise, and lemon juice, and season with salt and pepper. Pour this into the bowl with the fish and fold the two together, being careful not to break up the flakes much more. Taste and season again.

Brush each slice of bread with olive oil, and season lightly with salt. Put the slices on a cookie sheet or sheet pan in a single layer and toast in the oven for 5 minutes, or until they're crisp. Spoon the salad into a clean serving bowl, and serve the toast alongside.

3 smoked trout fillets (about $^1/_2$ pound total), skinned and flaked

2 small tart apples, cored and cut into matchsticks

1 handful of fresh chives, finely minced

2 celery stalks, minced

1 tablespoon grated fresh horseradish (about 1 inch)

$^1/_2$ cup sour cream

$^1/_2$ cup mayonnaise, homemade (see page 15) or store-bought

Juice of $^1/_2$ lemon

Kosher salt and freshly ground black pepper

12 thin pieces of dark brown or pumpernickel bread

$^1/_2$ cup extra-virgin olive oil

PORTUGUESE-STYLE SALT COD FRITTERS
THIS IS MY TAKE ON BACALAO.
I'VE SPIKED THE POTATO MIX WITH CHOPPED
PARSLEY AND CILANTRO, WHICH GIVES IT A VERY
FRESH, CLEAN FLAVOR, AND THEN QUICKLY
FRIED SMALL BALLS INTO CRISP,
GOLDEN FRITTERS

Portuguese-Style Salt Cod Fritters with Lemon and Olives

1 ¼ hours + an overnight soaking | Makes about 25 fritters

Cod was once one of the most valuable commodities in the world—it was *the* sustainable protein for most of Europe for about five hundred years. Before refrigeration, most of Europe survived on salted, air-dried cod fillets (salt cod) and Portugal has been one of the largest producers for hundreds of years.

When used in cooking, salt cod is first soaked to remove much of the salt. It is reconstituted in simmering milk enhanced with garlic and then used a million different ways: as a means of adding salt to food (similar to the way anchovies are used), folded into stews, or mixed with creamy, soft, cooked potatoes to form *bacalao,* the Portuguese national dish.

This is my take on bacalao. I've spiked the potato mix with chopped parsley and cilantro, which gives it a very fresh, clean flavor, and then quickly fried small balls into crisp, golden fritters. Squeeze fresh lemon over the top and you've got a fantastic hors d'oeuvre that's original and very easy to make.

1 pound dried, boneless salt cod

2 cups milk

3 garlic cloves

2 bay leaves

½ small bunch of fresh thyme

4 starchy potatoes, such as Idaho

1 large onion, finely chopped

2 garlic cloves, minced

1 handful of fresh flat-leaf parsley, chopped

1 handful of fresh cilantro, chopped

2 large eggs

1 to 2 tablespoons milk, as needed

Freshly ground black pepper

Kosher salt, if needed

Peanut oil, for frying

1 cup oil-cured black olives

Lemon wedges, for serving

Starting a day ahead, soak the dried cod in cold water for 18 to 24 hours, changing the water several times to remove the majority of the salt. Drain the cod, rinse, and put it in a large pot. Add the milk, garlic, bay leaves, thyme, and enough water to cover the cod by 1 inch; cooking the cod in milk keeps it very moist. Bring to a boil, then simmer gently over medium-low heat for 20 minutes, or until the cod is tender and pliable. Drain (discard the milk) and rinse the fish well, then flake it into a bowl, removing any little bits of skin and bone.

While the cod is cooking, put the potatoes in a pot with water to cover, bring to a boil, then simmer over medium heat for 20 to 25 minutes, until very tender. Drain the potatoes, peel, and mash them well in a bowl with a potato masher, or pass them through a ricer or sieve.

Add the cod to the bowl with the potatoes, along with the onion, minced garlic, parsley, cilantro, and eggs. Beat the mixture vigorously with a wooden spoon until it's really well combined and stiff; a spoon should stand up in it. (If it's too dry, add 1 or 2 tablespoons of milk.) Season with a pinch of pepper and taste for salt—you probably won't need to add any, as the cod itself is still salty in spite of having been soaked and boiled.

With lightly moistened hands or using two tablespoons, shape the cod mixture into egg-shaped balls—you should get about 25. (The cod balls can be covered and refrigerated for up to 1 day before cooking, or frozen in a tightly covered container for several weeks.)

Heat about 1 inch of oil in a deep, heavy skillet or pot to 370°F. on a deep-fry thermometer. Add a few of the fritters to the oil and cook, turning them three or four times to get them nicely browned all over. Carefully lift them out of the pan with a slotted spoon and drain on a platter lined with paper towels.. Keep going to cook all of the fritters. Taste one and, if needed, sprinkle with salt while the fritters are still hot. Serve hot or at room temperature with a pile of olives and lemon wedges.

Sautéed Feta Cheese

30 minutes | Serves 6 to 8

One summer I spent in France I fell in love with the pungent stink of the cheese shop in the town where my family and I were staying. I remember one firm sheep's cheese in particular that was marinated in these wonderful Mediterranean flavors, like capers, parsley, and anchovies. It was practically drowned in delicious olive oil and I had it almost every day for lunch.

Here's my version. It goes down great at a cocktail party and it really makes the chopped-herb sauce from page 21 sing.

Cut the feta into ½-inch-thick slices. Put the flour on a large plate. Put a large nonstick skillet over medium-high heat and coat with a 2-count of oil. When the oil is smoking, dredge the cheese slices in the flour, and add as many slices as will comfortably fit in the pan. Brown about 1 minute on each side, until golden brown. Squeeze some lemon juice over them, then use a spatula to carefully transfer to a platter. Repeat with the rest of the cheese, adding a little more oil to the pan if you need to. Spoon the chopped-herb sauce over the cheese and serve.

1 large block (1 ½ pounds) feta cheese
1 cup all-purpose flour
Extra-virgin olive oil
½ lemon
1 recipe Parsley, Raisin, Caper, and Pine Nut Sauce (page 21)

Swedish Meatballs with Lingonberry Sauce

1 hour 15 minutes + time to dry the bread crumbs | Makes 20 meatballs

1 cup fresh bread crumbs (see Note),
   spread out on a baking sheet for
   1 hour to dry at room temperature

¾ cup milk

6 tablespoons (¾ stick) unsalted
   butter

4 shallots, minced

2 garlic cloves, minced

1 teaspoon caraway seeds, toasted
   and ground

Kosher salt and freshly ground
   white pepper

1 pound ground beef

1 pound ground pork

1 large egg

1 handful of fresh flat-leaf parsley,
   chopped, plus more for garnish

1 handful of fresh dill, chopped

2 tablespoons all-purpose flour

1 ½ cups chicken stock, homemade
   (see page 36) or store-bought

¾ cup sour cream

¼ cup lingonberry or red currant
   jam, plus more for serving

Put the bread crumbs in a small bowl, add the milk, and stir with a fork. Let that stand for 5 minutes.

Put 3 tablespoons of the butter in a small skillet and let it melt over medium heat. Add the shallots, garlic, and caraway and season with salt and pepper. Sauté until the vegetables are softened but not browned, about 2 minutes. Get a large bowl and put the ground beef and pork into it. Add the cooked shallot mixture, the egg, the handful of parsley, and dill, and season with a fair amount of salt and pepper. Then squeeze the milk out of the soaked bread crumbs, add the bread crumbs to the bowl with the meat mixture, and mix well with your hands.

Now you're ready to make the meatballs. Moisten your hands to keep the meat from sticking. Then pinch off about ½ cup of the meat mixture and roll it around in your hands to shape it into a ball about the size of a cue ball. Put it on a platter. Keep on going until you've used all of the mixture. You should have about 20 meatballs.

Melt 2 more tablespoons of the butter in a large skillet over medium heat. When the foam starts to subside, add the meatballs (work in batches so you don't overcrowd the pan) and sauté, turning, until they're well browned on all sides, about 7 minutes for each batch. Remove the meatballs to a platter lined with paper towels.

The last thing to do is make the sauce. Pour off most of the fat from the skillet and return it to the heat. Add the remaining tablespoon of butter and swirl it around to coat the pan. Sprinkle in the flour and stir with a wooden spoon to dissolve the flour into the fat. Pour in the broth and stir with the spoon to loosen the bits from the bottom of the pan. Simmer, stirring, until the liquid is reduced and the mixture starts to thicken to a sauce. Season with salt and pepper. Lower the heat and stir in the sour cream. Stir in the jam and return the meatballs to the sauce. Simmer until the sauce thickens slightly and the meatballs are heated through, 15 to 20 minutes. Shower the whole thing with parsley.

To serve, spoon a couple of meatballs onto each plate along with a spoonful of sauce, and serve with additional jam on the side.

NOTE | For 1 cup of fresh bread crumbs, cut the crusts off of 3 slices of stale white bread, and pulse the bread in the food processor.

Baby Eggplants Stuffed with Lamb, Lemon, and Mint

1 1/2 hours | Makes 8 stuffed eggplants

Lamb and eggplant is a combination that travels across the culinary map from Northern Africa to the Mediterranean and the Middle East. This is my take on a Turkish dish of stuffed eggplants called *imam bayildi*—stuffed eggplant. If you can't find ground lamb, ground beef or pork will work just as well.

Using a paring knife, cut a wedge out of each eggplant, from stem to base, just large enough to stick a spoon inside. Scoop out the flesh and discard it.

Cover the bottom of a large sauté pan with a 2-count of oil and heat it just to the smoking point over medium heat. Add the eggplants in a single layer and fry on all sides until slightly charred and blistered. Remove to a platter and set aside.

Now return the pan to the heat. Add a little more oil if the pan is dry. Throw in the shallots and garlic and sauté for 5 minutes, until the vegetables are soft and golden brown. Add the ground lamb and brown the meat well, breaking it up with a wooden spoon as you're cooking it. There shouldn't be any pink left. Stir in the tomatoes and let the whole thing simmer for 5 minutes. Season with salt and pepper. Toss in all but 2 tablespoons of the parsley, all of the mint, and the lemon juice and stir it all together. Continue cooking for 2 to 3 minutes. Remove the pan from the heat and let the stuffing cool a bit.

Preheat the oven to 350°F. When the stuffing is cool enough to handle, spoon it into the eggplants; they should feel full, but not overly packed. Arrange the eggplants in a single layer in a large saucepan and pour the chicken stock over. Lay the lemon slices on top and drizzle with some more olive oil. Bake for 20 to 30 minutes, or until the eggplants are tender enough to cut with a fork. Garnish with the rest of the parsley before serving.

8 baby eggplants, each about the size of a lemon

1/4 cup extra-virgin olive oil

3 shallots, minced

2 garlic cloves, minced

1 pound ground lamb

2 medium, ripe tomatoes, peeled and chopped

Kosher salt and freshly ground black pepper

1/2 small bunch of fresh flat-leaf parsley, chopped

1 tablespoon chopped fresh mint

Juice of 1/2 lemon

3/4 cup chicken stock, homemade (see page 36) or store-bought

1 lemon, sliced paper-thin

Field Mushrooms Roasted with Sausage and Raisins

45 minutes + 1 hour to dry the bread crumbs | Makes 2 dozen stuffed mushrooms

This is a riff on the old idea of stuffed mushrooms—just updated with lots of great flavor that really complements the taste of fresh pork. I've always gone for ground pork that has a decent amount of fat running through it; when it cooks, the fat melts through the salty olives and sweet raisins and makes the mushrooms taste truly amazing.

¹/₄ **cup raisins**

¹/₂ **cup chopped large Spanish green olives**

¹/₄ **cup pine nuts**

2 handfuls of fresh flat-leaf parsley

1 pound Italian sausage, removed from casings and crumbled

1 cup freshly grated Pecorino cheese, plus more for garnish

Extra-virgin olive oil

Kosher salt and freshly ground black pepper

Pinch of dried red pepper flakes

24 large white mushrooms, stems removed

1 cup fresh bread crumbs (see Note), dried on a baking sheet at room temperature for about 1 hour

Preheat the oven to 500° F.

First make the stuffing. Combine the raisins, olives, pine nuts, and parsley on a cutting board, give it all a rough chop, and put it into a medium mixing bowl. Add the sausage and all but about 2 tablespoons of the cheese. Drizzle with a little oil. Add a pinch of salt and pepper, and the red pepper flakes. Mix it all together with your hands.

Oil the bottom and sides of a baking dish large enough to hold all of the mushrooms in a single layer (an earthenware dish looks cool for serving). Arrange the mushrooms snugly in the dish, stem side up; season the insides with salt and pepper and drizzle with more olive oil. Stuff each mushroom with a generous spoonful of the sausage stuffing. In a small bowl, stir the bread crumbs with the reserved 2 tablespoons of cheese. Sprinkle this mixture over the mushrooms. Drizzle a little more olive oil all over the top. Roast the mushrooms until the stuffing is cooked, the tops are brown, and the mushrooms are tender, 15 to 20 minutes.

NOTE | For 1 cup of fresh bread crumbs, cut the crusts off of 3 slices of bread and pulse the bread in a food processor.

WAIT UNTIL YOUR FRIENDS TASTE THE CAVIAR
WITH THE CRISP POTATOES.
IT'S GOING TO KEEP THEM TALKING
FOR WEEKS.

Roasted Fingerling Potatoes with Crème Fraîche and Caviar

1 hour | Serves 6

When I buy caviar, I look first for either sevruga or golden osetra. Both are impressive and oceany without costing a ton. I don't want to give too much away, but wait until you taste the caviar with the crisp potatoes. It's going to keep them talking for weeks.

2 pounds fingerling potatoes, scrubbed and cut in half lengthwise

¼ cup plus 2 tablespoons extra-virgin olive oil

Needles from 1 sprig of fresh rosemary, chopped

Kosher salt and freshly ground black pepper

6 ounces crème fraîche

1 ounce sevruga or osetra caviar

Preheat the oven to 375°F.

In a large mixing bowl, toss the potatoes with ¼ cup of the oil, the rosemary, and a generous seasoning of salt and pepper. Coat a roasting pan with the remaining 2 tablespoons of olive oil. Now dump the potatoes out into the pan, and arrange them cut sides down (the cut surface will caramelize and get very crisp, like a potato chip). Give the pan a good shake so the potatoes don't stick to the pan, put it in the oven, and roast for 30 to 40 minutes, until the potatoes are crispy, brown, and tender.

Let the potatoes cool slightly. Then take a potato half and, holding it cut side up, spread it with about ¼ teaspoon crème fraîche and then ½ teaspoon caviar. Do the same for the rest of the potatoes, divide them among 6 plates, and serve warm. (Or serve the potatoes in a large bowl, with bowls of caviar and crème fraîche alongside for self-service.)

Salad of Roasted Beets and Arugula

20 minutes + roasting time | Serves 6

The beets taste like small earthy candy and, with the salty blue cheese, make a perfect bite. This is a great starter.

Start with the beets because they take awhile to roast. Preheat the oven to 400°F. Now you'll need to make a pouch using two 12-inch sheets of aluminum foil. Lay one piece of foil on your work surface and put the beets in the center. Drizzle with a 3-count of olive oil and sprinkle with the thyme, salt, and pepper. Cover with the second piece of foil and crimp the edges several times to seal the pouch. Put that in the oven and roast for about 1 hour, or until a knife goes smoothly into the beets. (You can stick the knife right through the foil.) Take the pouch out of the oven, open it up to let the beets cool, and then peel and cut each beet into four wedges. Put the beets in a large bowl, add the arugula, celery leaves, and walnuts, and toss it all together.

For the dressing, in a medium bowl whisk together the blue cheese, sour cream, lemon juice, and 2 tablespoons of water. Pour that over the salad and toss. Divide among 6 serving plates.

2 pounds baby beets (2 to 3 bunches), washed and trimmed
Extra-virgin olive oil
Leaves from 2 sprigs of fresh thyme
Kosher salt and freshly ground black pepper
5 cups arugula, washed, dried, and hand-torn
Leaves from 1/2 bunch of celery, chopped
1/2 cup walnuts
1/4 cup crumbled excellent-quality blue cheese
1/2 cup sour cream
2 tablespoons fresh lemon juice

Artichokes with Lemon, Sausage, and Sage

1 ¹/₂ hours | Serves 8

You'll find this dish served in homes in Florence throughout the Christmas holidays. It's an amalgamation of great flavors. The earthy sweet artichokes, the lemons, and sage act as supporting players to make the sausage taste amazing. This dish looks beautiful served on individual plates or passed around at the table on a big platter, family style.

First thing to do is to steam the artichokes in a flavorful broth. Put the parsley, garlic cloves, bay leaves, wine, and lemon halves in a wide pot. Add 2 quarts of water and bring to a simmer. Season the broth with salt and pepper.

While that's coming to a simmer, wash the artichokes under cold water. Then, using a paring knife, trim the bottom end of each stem and shave the stem down to expose the tender, light green flesh underneath. Snap or cut off the outer petals until you reach the soft, pale green leaves in the center. Slice off about 1 inch from the top of each artichoke with a large knife.

Slide the artichokes into the simmering broth, then cover the pan and simmer over medium-low heat for about 20 minutes, until there is no resistance when a knife is inserted into the base of each artichoke. Remove the artichokes from the broth with tongs. Using a spoon, carefully scoop out the hairy choke from the center of each and discard. Try to keep the artichoke intact as best you can; it looks great for presentation.

Now go on to the rest of the dish. Put a large, deep skillet over medium heat and cover the bottom with a 2-count of oil. When the oil is smoking hot, add the sausages and cook for 7 to 10 minutes, until cooked through and browned all over. Take the sausages out of the pan and set them aside. Add a drizzle of oil to the pan. Then add the sage leaves and cook for 2 to 3 minutes to infuse the oil with their flavor. Toss in the shallots, garlic, and lemon slices and cook for 2 minutes. Add the stock to the pan, bring to a boil, lower the heat, and simmer until reduced and thickened. Swirl in the butter to emulsify, and add a drizzle of olive oil for flavor. Return the artichokes to the pan and cook over low heat for a few minutes to warm them up. Spoon the artichokes out onto plates and serve with half a sausage.

ARTICHOKES

1 handful of fresh flat-leaf parsley

4 garlic cloves

2 bay leaves

¹/₄ cup dry white wine, such as Pinot Grigio

1 lemon, halved

Kosher salt and freshly ground black pepper

4 whole artichokes

Extra-virgin olive oil

4 pork sausages (6 ounces each)

4 fresh sage leaves

2 shallots, minced

4 garlic cloves, minced

¹/₂ lemon, cut into paper-thin slices

¹/₂ cup chicken stock, homemade (see page 36) or store-bought

2 tablespoons unsalted butter

Chopped fresh flat-leaf parsley, for garnish

Crispy Potato Pancakes with Cinnamon Apples and Fresh Thyme

1 ¹/₂ hours | Makes about 20 pancakes

I've had lots of bad potato pancakes in my day, but this recipe is foolproof. I'll put these up against any Jewish grandmother's, any day of the week.

PANCAKES

4 medium russet potatoes, peeled

2 medium onions

Kosher salt and freshly ground black pepper

4 fresh chives, finely chopped

2 large egg whites, lightly beaten

Vegetable oil, for frying

First make the apples.

To get pancakes with a really crisp outer crust, you need to dry out the potatoes and onions before cooking so that they brown well. Using a box grater or food processor, coarsely grate the potatoes and onions. Put the vegetables together in a length of cheesecloth or a tea towel and twist it to squeeze out as much of the excess liquid as you can. Then dump the grated vegetables into a bowl and season with salt and pepper. Stir in the chives. Fold in the egg whites to bind the mixture together.

Preheat the oven to 200°F. Heat ¼ inch of oil in a large nonstick skillet over medium heat. Drop about 2 tablespoons of the potato mixture into the hot oil and use a spatula to gently flatten it into a thin pancake about 4 inches in diameter. You want them to fry up thin and crispy. Add another couple of pancakes to the pan, if there's room. Fry for 3 to 4 minutes on each side, until golden. Use a spatula to carefully lift the pancakes out of the pan, and drain on a platter lined with paper towels. Season with salt while the pancakes are still hot and put them in the oven to keep them hot. Continue frying, adding more oil as needed, until all of the mixture is used.

Apples with Cinnamon and Thyme

3 McIntosh apples, cored and sliced | Juice of ¹/₂ lemon | ¹/₄ cup water | 1 cinnamon stick | 2 sprigs of fresh thyme

Put everything into a pot over medium-low heat and cook, uncovered, until the apples soften and the water evaporates, about 15 minutes. Take the pan off the heat and let cool while you make the pancakes. Remove the thyme sprigs before serving.

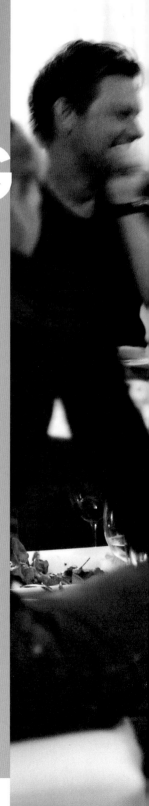

NOSHING

When everyone piles into my kitchen—which is more often than not—I'll **THROW TOGETHER LARGE PLATTERS** of tasty stuff and a big handful of forks. Completely informal occasions like this usually happen outside of normal mealtimes, and **GRAZING IS THE ORDER OF THE MOMENT.** This chapter is full of simple recipes—almost improvisational cooking—that can be put together at a moment's notice. **BIG FLAVORS** like cold sesame noodles; crispy, fried Chinese salt-and-pepper prawns; a big bowl of guacamole and fresh, warm tortilla chips. Big platters of food or a series of small appetizers (what the Greeks call *mezze*) have global appeal, **LOTS OF WOW FACTOR,** and take noshing to a whole new level.

Brandade with Parsley Toast

1 ¼ hours + an overnight soaking | Serves 4 to 6

Starting a day ahead, soak the dried cod in cold water for 18 to 24 hours, changing the water several times to remove the majority of the salt. Drain the cod, rinse, and put it in a large pot. Add the milk, 5 garlic cloves, bay leaves, thyme, and enough water to cover the cod by 1 inch; cooking the cod in milk keeps it very moist. Bring it to a boil, reduce the heat, and simmer gently for 20 minutes, or until the cod is tender and pliable. Drain the cod, reserving the garlic, and rinse the cod well. Then flake the cod into a bowl, removing any little bits of skin and bone that you come across. Discard the milk, bay leaves, and thyme.

While the cod is cooking, put the potatoes in a pot, cover them with water, and simmer over medium heat for 20 to 25 minutes, until very tender. Drain the potatoes and peel off the skin, then mash them well with a potato masher or pass them through a ricer or sieve into a large bowl.

Preheat the oven to 250°F. Arrange the baguette slices on one or two sheet pans in a single layer. Sprinkle with parsley and drizzle with olive oil. Toast slowly in the oven until nice and crispy, 20 to 25 minutes.

To put it all together, combine the flaked cod, the cooked garlic, olive oil, cream, lemon juice, and ground pepper to the bowl with the potatoes. Whip with an electric mixer until the mixture is well combined and lightened. Taste for salt; you probably won't need any. Put the brandade into a big serving bowl, and finish with a drizzle of olive oil and freshly ground pepper. Rub the toasts with the raw garlic and serve alongside.

1 ½ pounds dried, boneless salt cod

1 quart milk

5 garlic cloves, plus 2 to 3 for seasoning the baguette slices

2 bay leaves

½ bunch of fresh thyme

2 medium Idaho potatoes

1 baguette, thinly sliced

½ bunch of fresh flat-leaf parsley, chopped

¼ cup extra-virgin olive oil, plus extra for drizzling

½ cup heavy cream

Juice of ½ lemon, or more to taste

Kosher salt and freshly ground black pepper

Fritto Misto of Sea Creatures

45 minutes | Serves 8 to 10

The best *fritto misto* I ever ate was served to me in the little seaside town of Ventimiglia on the Ligurian coast of Italy, right across the border from France. We stopped there for lunch one day and had a bottle of wine and a plateful of strange, fried Mediterranean creatures (*rouget, rascasse,* and the like) that had just been pulled from the ocean that morning. The fish were very simply served: crispy, with fresh sea salt and a little squeeze of lemon. The seafood in the recipe below should be a little more familiar to you.

1 pound squid, bodies only

3 cups milk

3 large eggs

12 fresh basil leaves

1 pound shrimp, peeled

1 pound whole baby octopus, cleaned
(optional)

1/2 pound fresh, whole sardines

Canola oil, for frying

3 cups all-purpose flour

Kosher salt and freshly ground
black pepper

Lemon wedges, for serving

Rinse the squid under cool water and pat dry with paper towels. Cut the bodies into 1/4-inch rings.

Combine the milk, eggs, and basil leaves in a bowl and mix with a fork until lightly beaten. Pour about one third of the batter into another smaller bowl and add the squid. Put all the rest of the seafood in the other bowl of batter and stick both in the fridge while you get everything else set up. The seafood fries better if marinated and chilled for about 15 minutes.

Preheat the oven to 200°F. Pour about 2 inches of oil into a deep-fryer or a large, heavy pot and heat to 375°F. on a deep-fry thermometer. Put the flour in a pie plate and season with a fair amount of salt and pepper. Fry the squid first. Working in batches, toss the squid in the seasoned flour to coat, pat off the excess, and fry for 2 to 3 minutes, until golden brown. Using a slotted spoon, transfer the fried squid to paper towels to drain. Season with salt while still hot and keep warm in the oven. Now flour and fry the second bowl of seafood just like you did the squid; it will take 3 to 4 minutes per batch. Season with salt and serve while it's still hot, with lemon wedges.

Carpaccio of Beef with Crushed Grape Tomatoes and Horseradish

30 minutes + about 2 hours to chill the meat | Serves 6 to 8

This is kind of a showstopper when you have people coming over. It looks fantastic on the plate and the flavors are really clean. The thin-sliced raw beef tastes rich with a sharp, peppery crust; the tomatoes are sweet; and the horseradish is creamy. Excellent.

Roll the tenderloin in the cracked pepper just to give it a very light coating; too much pepper will make the beef taste bitter. Now put a large, heavy skillet over medium-high heat. Add a 2-count drizzle of oil and get it smoking hot. Put the tenderloin in the skillet and sear the outside of the meat all over, leaving the inside raw, 5 to 8 minutes total. Take the meat out of the pan, wrap it in plastic, and refrigerate until it gets good and cold, 1 to 2 hours.

While you wait for the beef to chill, stir the horseradish, sour cream, lemon juice, and olive oil together in a bowl. Season it up with salt and pepper.

When the beef is cold, use a long, very sharp knife to cut the meat into slices as thin as you can make them. Lay them out on a platter (they'll overlap—that's fine). Now drizzle the horseradish sauce all over the meat. Hand-crush the tomatoes in a bowl and add olive oil to make them saucy; season that with salt and pepper too so that it tastes really good. Drizzle that over the top and garnish the whole thing with watercress.

2 pounds beef tenderloin

$1/4$ cup freshly cracked black peppercorns (use the bottom of a pot to crack them)

Extra-virgin olive oil

$1/2$ cup grated fresh horseradish

1 cup sour cream

Juice of 1 lemon

2 tablespoons extra-virgin olive oil

Kosher salt and freshly ground black pepper

1 pint grape tomatoes, halved

$1/4$ cup olive oil

Watercress sprigs, for garnish

Pizza

the ancient city of Pompeii outside Naples, they uncovered what was presumed to be a bakery district. And there, encapsulated in the lava, were perfectly preserved round disks of baked flatbread. More recently, scientists did DNA testing on the bread and found that it was made of milled wheat and seawater, not too terribly different from the delicious pizza you can still find in Naples. Resident Pompeiians pressed salted anchovies to extract the oil, then drizzled the anchovy oil over the disks of flatbread to make an early form of what we'd call anchovy pizza.

I love anchovies on my pizza, I love *mozzarella di bufala*, I love fresh basil, I love sausage, I love ricotta cheese. And every time I make fresh pizza dough I feel like I'm touching history.

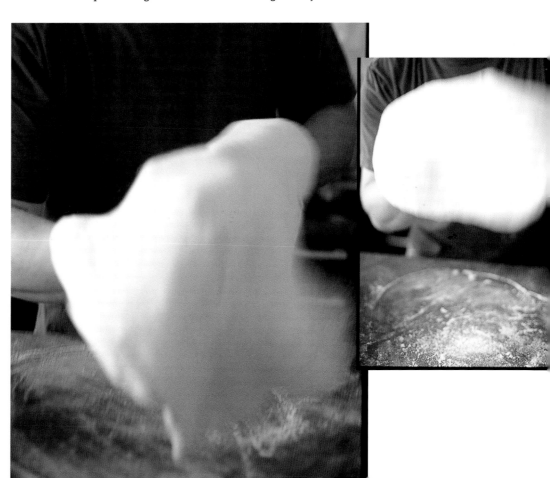

Fresh Pizza Dough

**20 minutes + 1 hour for rising | Makes enough for 1 large
(14- to 15-inch) pizza**

Fresh pizza dough is actually one of the easiest recipes in this book. You can bake it on a pizza stone if you have one, to make thin, crisp-crusted pizza. Or just press the dough into a sheet pan, drizzle it with olive oil, and sprinkle with fresh rosemary to make focaccia; it's the same recipe.

1 package active dry yeast

1 teaspoon sugar

1 cup warm (100°F. to 110°F.) water

1 tablespoon kosher salt

2 tablespoons extra-virgin olive oil

3 cups unbleached all-purpose flour,
  plus more for dusting

In the bowl of a standing electric mixer fitted with a dough hook, or in a mixing bowl, combine the yeast, sugar, and warm water and stir gently to dissolve. Let the mixture stand until the yeast comes alive and starts to foam, 5 to 10 minutes.

If you're using a mixer, turn the mixer on low and add the salt and the 2 tablespoons of olive oil. Add the flour, a little at a time, mixing at the lowest speed until all the flour has been incorporated. When the dough starts to come together, increase the speed to medium and let it go until the dough gathers into a ball. This should take about 5 minutes. Stop the machine periodically to scrape the dough off the hook. Get a feel for the dough as you're making it by squeezing a small amount together between your thumb and fingers. If it's crumbly, add more water; if it's sticky, add more flour, 1 tablespoon at a time. Turn the dough out onto a lightly floured surface and fold it over itself a few times, kneading until it's smooth and elastic.

If you're making the dough by hand, stir in the salt and the 2 tablespoons of olive oil. Then begin stirring in the flour. When the mixture becomes too stiff to stir with the spoon, knead the rest of the flour in by hand, adding just enough so that the dough is soft but not sticky. As you work, squeeze a small amount of dough together between your thumb and fingers. If it's crumbly, add more water; if it's sticky, add more flour, 1 tablespoon at a time. Knead until smooth and elastic, about 10 minutes.

Form the dough into a round and put it into a lightly oiled bowl, turning it over to coat the dough entirely with the oil. Cover with plastic wrap or a damp towel and let it rise in a warm spot (i.e., over a gas pilot light) until doubled in size, about 1 hour.

Grilled Pizza with Mozzarella di Bufala, Sausage, and Fresh Tomatoes

About 2 hours, including rising time for the dough | Serves 4 to 6

Grilling gives pizza a nice charred, smoky flavor like some of the pizzas you get in restaurants in New York City. I take all the topping ingredients and toss them in a bowl, then slather them over the warm pizza crust, sticky with olive oil, and let the heat from the crust just warm the cheese through. Mozzarella di Bufala is mozzarella that is made with the milk of water buffalo. You can buy it, imported, packed in water.

Make the pizza dough and let it rise. Once the dough is domed and spongy, turn it out onto a lightly floured counter. Roll and stretch the dough into a cylinder. Cover and let rest for 15 minutes so it will be easier to roll out. In the meantime, get going on the pizza topping.

Preheat an outdoor gas or charcoal grill and get it very hot. Take a few paper towels and fold them several times to make a thick square. Blot a small amount of oil on the paper towels. Then carefully and quickly wipe the hot grates of the grill to make a nonstick grilling surface. Grill the sausages until cooked through, turning with tongs. Set aside. Keep the grill hot to make the pizza.

Crush the tomatoes in your hands into a bowl. Add the garlic and basil. Crumble in the sausage. Rip the mozzarella into pieces with your hands and add that too along with a glug-glug of olive oil; season with salt and pepper. Mix that up with your hands; it'll be like a big salad. Taste for seasoning and add more olive oil if needed.

On a lightly floured pizza paddle, roll or pat out the dough into a rustic, oblong shape about $1/2$ inch thick. Brush the crust with a thin layer of olive oil, sprinkle with salt, and lay it oil side down onto the hot grill. Once the dough looks set, about 2 minutes, turn the crust over carefully with tongs. Close the grill cover and cook the crust until golden and crisp, 2 to 3 more minutes. Transfer the crust to a platter. Scoop the fresh tomato–mozzarella salad up in your hands and spread it over the top. Sprinkle with a good dusting of Parmigiano-Reggiano cheese and finish with a drizzle of olive oil.

1 recipe Fresh Pizza Dough
  (page 80)
Extra-virgin olive oil
1 $1/2$ pounds sweet Italian sausage,
  in links
1 $1/2$ pints red cherry tomatoes
1 $1/2$ pints yellow cherry tomatoes
2 garlic cloves, minced
Leaves from 1 bunch of fresh basil,
  torn into pieces
2 (8-ounce) balls of fresh Mozzarella
  di Bufala, drained
Kosher salt and freshly ground
  black pepper
1 cup freshly grated Parmigiano-
  Reggiano cheese

White Clam Pizza

About 2 hours, including rising time for the dough | Makes 1 large (14- to 15-inch) pizza

I ate this pizza on a boardwalk in Atlantic City. It reminded me of the old classic, Clams Casino. The bacon, the clams, and the cheese still taste great together.

1 recipe Fresh Pizza Dough
    (page 80)
2 dozen large hard-shell clams, such
    as cherrystone or chowder
Kosher salt and freshly ground
    black pepper
4 bay leaves
Juice of $1/2$ lemon
Extra-virgin olive oil
1 medium onion, chopped
1 red bell pepper, cored, seeded,
    and chopped
2 garlic cloves, chopped
2 to 3 medium-size ripe tomatoes,
    seeded and chopped
Leaves from 2 sprigs of fresh oregano
All-purpose flour, for rolling
Cornmeal, for dusting
1 (15-ounce) container ricotta
    cheese
$1/4$ pound bacon, cut in 1-inch pieces
1 handful of fresh flat-leaf parsley,
    chopped
$1/2$ cup freshly grated Pecorino
    cheese

Make the dough and let it rise.

Meanwhile, wash and scrub the clams well under cold running water to remove the sand. Combine 1 inch of water, $1/2$ teaspoon salt, and 2 of the bay leaves in a steamer or large pot. Cover and bring to a simmer. Add the clams, cover, and steam for 5 to 10 minutes until the clams open; discard any that do not. Remove the clams from their shells and coarsely chop them. Put them in a bowl, add the lemon juice and a drizzle of olive oil, and season with salt and pepper. Set that aside while you make the rest of the stuff that goes on top.

This is a good time to stick a big pizza stone in the oven and preheat the oven to 500°F.

Coat a sauté pan with a 2-count of olive oil, put it over medium heat, and get it hot. Add the onion, bell pepper, garlic, and tomatoes. Toss in the remaining 2 bay leaves and the oregano. Cook, stirring, until the vegetables have cooked down and are good and soft, about 10 minutes. Season with salt and pepper and take the pan off the heat.

Once the dough is domed and spongy, turn it out onto a lightly floured counter. Roll and stretch the dough out to a large circle, about $1/2$ inch thick. Dust a pizza paddle with cornmeal and slide it under the pizza dough. Spread the ricotta evenly over the crust with the back of a spoon. Scatter the chopped clams all around and top with the red pepper–tomato mixture. Distribute the pieces of bacon on top and shower with about half of the parsley. Drizzle with olive oil. Turn the oven temperature down to 475°F. and slide the pizza onto the hot stone. Bake for 12 to 15 minutes, until the crust is golden and crisp and the ricotta is bubbly.

Before cutting the pizza into slices, grate Pecorino over the whole thing and shower with the remaining chopped parsley. Finish with a drizzle of oil.

Pizza with Roasted Mushrooms, Spinach, and Goat Cheese

About 2 hours, including rising time for the dough | Makes 1 large (14- to 15-inch) pizza

Five perfect tastes in one bite: earthy mushrooms, salty prosciutto, fresh rosemary, crispy pizza, and the sharp bite of the goat cheese . . . delicious.

Make the pizza dough and let it rise.

Preheat the oven to 500°F. and put a big pizza stone in the oven to heat.

In the meantime, coat a sauté pan with a 2-count of olive oil. Put it over medium heat and get it hot. Add the prosciutto strips and stir for a minute or so to release the fat and flavor. Toss in the garlic and rosemary and cook for about 30 seconds. Then drizzle in some more oil, add the mushrooms, and season with salt and pepper. Cook, stirring, until the mushrooms have released their moisture and are nicely browned, about 5 minutes. Taste for salt and pepper and take the pan off the heat.

Check the dough: Once it's domed and spongy, turn it out onto a lightly floured counter. Roll and stretch the dough out to a large circle, about $1/2$ inch thick. Dust a pizza paddle with cornmeal and slide it under the pizza dough. Spread the goat cheese evenly over the dough with the back of a spoon (or crumble, if using aged). Scatter the sautéed mushrooms all around. Spread the spinach over that and top with the shredded Fontina. Lay a rosemary sprig across the center for a great presentation. Reduce the oven heat to 475°F. Slide the pizza onto the hot stone in the oven and bake for 12 to 15 minutes, until the crust is golden and crisp and the cheese is bubbly.

Grate Pecorino over the whole thing, then cut into slices.

1 recipe Fresh Pizza Dough (page 80)

Extra-virgin olive oil

2 slices prosciutto, cut into strips

2 garlic cloves, chopped

Needles from 1 fresh rosemary sprig, plus 1 sprig for garnish

1 pound assorted wild mushrooms, such as crimini, portobello, shiitake, oyster, and morel (or whatever you can find in the supermarket), cleaned and coarsely chopped

Kosher salt and freshly ground black pepper

All-purpose flour, for rolling

Cornmeal, for dusting

8 ounces fresh or aged goat cheese

1 bunch of fresh baby spinach, coarsely chopped

2 cups shredded Fontina cheese

$1/2$ cup freshly grated Pecorino cheese

African-Spiced Chicken with Green Olive Sauce and Couscous

1 hour 45 minutes + 30 minutes to marinate | Serves 6

I like to make this for a picnic because it packs up really well. The components all get wrapped up in flatbread. And it's great with champagne.

1 free-range chicken (3^1/$_2$ pounds)

1 recipe North African Spice Mix (page 27)

1 lemon, halved

^{1}/$_4$ bunch of fresh cilantro

1 head of garlic, halved horizontally

3 tablespoons extra-virgin olive oil

Freshly ground black pepper

APRICOT COUSCOUS

1 cup couscous

1^1/$_2$ cups cold water

10 dried apricots

^{1}/$_4$ cup whole almonds, toasted at 375˚F. for about 10 minutes

2 green onions, green parts only, sliced

2 handfuls of fresh mint leaves

2 handfuls of fresh cilantro leaves

Juice of ^{1}/$_2$ lemon

2 tablespoons extra-virgin olive oil

Kosher salt and freshly ground black pepper

GREEN OLIVE SAUCE

Extra-virgin olive oil

3 shallots, sliced

1 fresh red chile, split lengthwise

^{1}/$_2$ pound large green Spanish olives, pitted

^{1}/$_4$ bunch of fresh flat-leaf parsley, stemmed

2 tablespoons sherry vinegar

Juice of ^{1}/$_2$ lemon

4 lavash breads or pitas

Preheat the oven to 400˚F.

Rinse the chicken inside and out with cool water, then pat it dry with paper towels. Massage the chicken skin with the spice mix—make sure you don't miss a spot. Now stuff the lemon halves, cilantro, and garlic into the cavity and put the chicken in a roasting pan fitted with a rack. Fold the wing tips under the bird and tie the legs together with kitchen string. Drizzle the oil all over the chicken and season with pepper. If you have time, let the chicken marinate for 30 minutes in the fridge to really get the flavors down deep into the meat. Roast the chicken for 1 hour. Pop an instant-read thermometer into the thickest part of the thigh. When it reads 160˚F., the chicken's done.

While the bird is cooking, make the couscous. Put the couscous into a medium bowl. Pour the water over it and stir with a fork. Cover and let it sit for 10 to15 minutes, then fluff with a fork. Put the apricots, almonds, green onions, mint, and cilantro on a cutting board and coarsely chop everything up. Add this to the couscous. Then add the lemon juice and olive oil, and season with salt and pepper. Toss gently.

When the chicken is done, let it rest for 20 minutes so the juices can settle back into the meat and the chicken cools down a bit. Then pull off and discard the skin. Pull the lemon halves out of the cavity and set them aside; you'll need them. Pull the meat from the bones and shred it with your fingers or two forks. Put the shredded chicken in a large bowl and squeeze the reserved lemon halves over to moisten.

Now you're ready to move on to the green olive sauce: Put a small skillet over low heat and add a 2-count of olive oil. Add the shallots and chile and cook for 8 minutes, stirring, until caramelized. Scrape that into the bowl of a food processor. Add the olives, parsley, vinegar, lemon juice, and ^{1}/$_2$ cup of olive oil. Purée for a good 3 minutes, until totally smooth.

To put the whole thing together, tear off pieces of the lavash bread in big, fat strips. Put some of the shredded chicken and couscous on the lavash, add a few spoonfuls of the olive sauce, and roll the sandwiches up.

Grilled Octopus from a Small Restaurant in Nice

1 hour 45 minutes | Serves 6

Just behind the farmers' market in Nice, along one of those cobblestoned back streets, there's a restaurant called Le Zoo. It serves amazing pizzas with salty anchovies and pesto and, of course, this dish of grilled octopus, a Mediterranean staple. The octopus is poached with garlic and lemon until soft, then grilled until the outside starts to char and crisp slightly. The octopus tastes sweet and of the ocean, and the chopped fennel and tomato sauce tastes as amazing as the French Mediterranean is blue.

Put the octopus into a pot with the garlic, lemon halves, salt, and water to cover. Bring to a boil, reduce the heat, and simmer until the octopus is very tender, about 1 hour and 15 minutes. Drain. Then cut the head off just below the eyes and discard; cut the tentacles apart. With your fingers, peel off any skin that's become slimy, or is loose.

In a small bowl, stir the lemon zest and celery into the chopped-herb sauce.

Put a large grill pan on two burners over medium-high heat or preheat an outdoor gas or charcoal grill and get it very hot. Take a few paper towels and fold them several times to make a thick square. Blot a small amount of oil on the paper towels, then carefully and quickly wipe the hot grates of the grill to make a nonstick grilling surface. With more paper towels, pat the cooked octopus tentacles dry and toss in a bowl with olive oil, salt, and pepper. Grill the tentacles all over until they're nice and crisp, 3 to 4 minutes. Take them off the grill and cut them into 1- to 2-inch pieces. Serve with the sauce.

1 octopus, about 5 pounds, cleaned

1 head of garlic, cut in half horizontally

1 lemon, cut in half

Kosher salt and freshly ground black pepper

Grated zest of 1 lemon

$1/4$ cup chopped celery

1 recipe Basil, Olive, Tomato, and Fennel Sauce (page 23)

Extra-virgin olive oil

Salt-and-Pepper Prawns

1 hour | Serves 4 to 6

The greatest thing about Hong Kong is eating in the street markets of Kowloon, across Victoria Harbor from Hong Kong Island. Kowloon is where the real Chinese people live, and for a food lover, it's an eating experience you should not miss.

We got a recommendation to go see this guy in Kowloon. He had a make-shift kitchen in his stall (a bit unsanitary but really interesting) comprised basically of a wok. In front of the wok were large Styrofoam coolers filled with water and aerated with plastic tubes, holding all sorts of live seafood including stuff I'd never seen before, like a half-crab/half-shrimp creature. You point to the critter you want, he picks it up, and with four lightning-quick chops of the cleaver, it heads straight to the smoking-hot wok. This recipe for tempura fried shrimp with chiles and garlic is from his stall. I ate the entire plate sitting at a communal table covered by a plastic tablecloth, drinking a beer I'd never heard the name of. It was straight out of a Wong Kar-Wai movie.

BATTER

4 large egg yolks

4 to 4$\frac{1}{2}$ cups chilled soda water

4 cups all-purpose flour

Peanut oil, for deep-frying

1 to 2 cups all-purpose flour, for dredging

Kosher salt and freshly ground black pepper

2 pounds extra-large shrimp, shelled (leaving tail section attached) and deveined

2 tablespoons thinly sliced garlic

2 tablespoons shredded ginger

1 bunch of green onions, thinly sliced on an angle

1 jalapeño, sliced into rounds, with seeds

Lemon wedges, for serving

In a large mixing bowl, lightly beat the egg yolks with a fork until smooth, then pour in the soda water and stir to combine. Slowly add the flour and continue to mix with the fork until the batter is smooth and the consistency of heavy cream, adding more water if needed.

Pour 2 inches of oil into a wok or heavy pot and heat to 375°F. on a deep-fry thermometer. Put the flour on a platter and season it well with salt and pepper. Mix with your fingers to incorporate the seasoning.

Working in batches, first dredge the shrimp in the flour, then, holding them by the tails, dip them in the batter up to the tails. Let the excess batter drip off. Slide the shrimp into the hot oil and cook for about 3 minutes, or until golden brown. Use a spider or slotted spoon to turn the shrimp once during cooking. Then remove them from the oil and drain on paper towels. As you work, scoop out any floating bits of batter from the oil; they will burn. Season the shrimp with salt and pepper while they're still hot and put them on a serving platter.

Cook the remaining shrimp the same way and transfer to a serving platter. When all of the shrimp have been cooked, carefully pour out all but about 2 tablespoons of oil from the wok or pot into a safe container. Add the garlic, ginger, green onions, and jalapeño and cook, stirring, until crisp, about 1 minute. (Stand back—the green onions will spit when they hit the hot oil.) Scrape that out on top of the shrimp and serve with lemon wedges.

Cold Sesame Noodles

30 minutes | Serves 4

This is a classic Chinese take-out dish from my neighborhood in New York City. I used to order it all the time from restaurants until I figured out how easy it is to make. This dish traditionally uses Chinese egg noodles, but the sauce is really good with soba noodles or even angel-hair pasta.

Cook the noodles in a large pot of unsalted boiling water until barely tender and still firm, 3 to 4 minutes. Drain immediately and rinse under cold running water to cool. Drain the noodles really well and transfer to a wide serving bowl. Toss immediately with the sesame oil so they don't stick together.

Now make the sauce. In the same pot, heat the peanut oil over medium-low heat. Add the green onions, ginger, garlic, and chile paste. Cook, stirring, until the vegetables are soft and fragrant, about 1 minute. Then stir in the brown sugar, peanut butter, vinegar, soy sauce, and hot water. Keep stirring until the sugar is dissolved and the peanut butter has smoothed out. Now throw the noodles back into the pot and toss in the peanut sauce until well coated.

You're almost finished. Toast the sesame seeds in a dry skillet over medium-low heat until golden brown. (Shake the pan constantly to keep the seeds from burning.) Put the noodles back in the serving bowl, sprinkle with the sesame seeds, cucumber, green onion, cilantro, and nori, and serve. (You can also stick the sauced noodles in the refrigerator and serve them chilled.)

$^1/_2$ **pound fresh Chinese egg noodles**

3 tablespoons dark sesame oil

2 tablespoons peanut oil

2 green onions, thinly sliced on the diagonal

1-inch piece of fresh ginger, minced

3 garlic cloves, minced

1 teaspoon red chile paste, such as sambal

2 tablespoons brown sugar

$^1/_2$ **cup creamy peanut butter**

3 tablespoons rice vinegar

3 tablespoons low-sodium soy sauce

6 tablespoons hot water

1 tablespoon sesame seeds

Cucumber slices

Sliced green onion

Fresh cilantro leaves

Julienned nori strips

Thai Grilled Beef and Green Papaya Salad

45 minutes + time to marinate the beef | **Serves 4 to 6**

These are classic Thai flavors. If you can't find green papaya, shred a couple of cucumbers and it will work just as well. If you're using wooden skewers, soak them in water for about 20 minutes before you skewer the beef so that they don't catch fire on the grill. And try to find sambal for the chile paste.

First, slice the beef as thin as possible against the grain. Skewer and put the skewers in a shallow baking dish. Then stir together the soy sauce, vinegar, garlic, chile paste, and sugar; pour it over the beef; and marinate in the refrigerator for 1 hour. Turn the meat in the marinade at least once during the hour.

In the meantime, throw all of the ingredients for the dressing together in a bowl and whisk to combine.

Put a large grill pan on two burners over medium-high heat or preheat an outdoor gas or charcoal grill and get it very hot. Take a few paper towels and fold them several times to make a thick square. Blot a small amount of oil on the paper towels. Then carefully and quickly wipe the hot grates of the grill to make a nonstick grilling surface. Grill the beef on the skewers for about 1 minute on each side.

Shred the papaya, toss with the dressing, and mound it in a serving bowl. Scatter the cucumber, onion, bean sprouts, herbs, and peanuts over and season to taste with salt and pepper. Set the beef skewers alongside.

BEEF SKEWERS

1 pound beef sirloin

$1/4$ cup low-sodium soy sauce

$1/4$ cup rice vinegar

1 tablespoon chopped garlic

2 teaspoons chile paste

1 tablespoon brown sugar

DRESSING

$1/4$ cup rice vinegar

Juice of 1 lime

$1/2$ tablespoon chopped garlic

$1/2$ tablespoon chile paste

1 tablespoon sugar

$1 1/2$ tablespoons peanut oil

1 tablespoon Thai fish sauce (nam pla)

PAPAYA SALAD

1 green papaya (about $1 1/2$ pounds)

1 seedless cucumber, peeled and cut into julienne

$1/2$ red onion, thinly sliced

1 cup bean sprouts

$1/4$ cup fresh mint leaves

$1/4$ cup fresh cilantro leaves

2 tablespoons chopped unsalted peanuts, toasted

Kosher salt and freshly ground black pepper

Guacamole

20 minutes + 1 hour resting time | Makes about 4 cups

Many guacamole recipes do a disservice to avocados. When it's really simple—just avocados, chiles, lime juice, and salt—it's outstanding.

Halve and pit the avocados. With a tablespoon, scoop out the flesh into a mixing bowl. Mash the avocados with a fork, leaving them still a bit chunky. Add all of the rest of the ingredients, and fold everything together.

Lay a piece of plastic wrap right on the surface of the guacamole so it doesn't brown and refrigerate for at least 1 hour before serving.

10 ripe avocados

Juice of 3 limes

1 large onion, chopped

1 garlic clove, minced

2 serrano chiles, thinly sliced

1 big handful of fresh cilantro, finely chopped

Kosher salt and freshly ground black pepper

Fresh Tortilla Chips

45 minutes | Makes about 50 chips

Fresh tortilla chips are as delicious as they are uncomplicated to make. Warm chips with a big bowl of guacamole—that's probably what I'll choose for my last meal on the planet.

Heat the oil to 365°F. (on a frying thermometer) in a deep-fat fryer or a large, deep pot. Slide a good handful of the tortilla quarters into the hot oil. When they pop up to the top of the oil, cook for about 40 seconds on each side, turning once, until crisp and golden brown. Use a slotted spoon to transfer to a baking sheet lined with paper towels. Sprinkle with salt while the chips are still hot. When you have fried all of the chips, put them in a big serving bowl and serve with Guacamole (recipe above), Pico de Gallo (page 96), and Farmstand Salsa (page 96).

2 quarts canola oil

1 (14-ounce) package corn tortillas, cut into quarters

Kosher salt

Pico de Gallo

20 minutes | Makes 2 cups

Pico de gallo gets its light, bright flavor from the crisp texture of the vegetables, so you want to make sure they are evenly chopped and super-fresh. Don't stir the salsa too much when you're mixing it together. It should be the consistency of a relish, not mushy.

8 ripe tomatoes, chopped

2 small red onions, chopped

4 green onions, white and green parts, sliced

3 serrano chiles, thinly sliced

1 handful of fresh cilantro, chopped

4 garlic cloves, minced

Juice of 4 limes

$\frac{1}{4}$ cup extra-virgin olive oil

1 teaspoon kosher salt

Freshly ground black pepper

$\frac{1}{2}$ teaspoon ground cumin (toasted, if you have it; see Note)

Put all of the ingredients into a mixing bowl and stir it all together. Let sit for 15 minutes to allow the flavors to marry.

NOTE | To make toasted ground cumin, put a few tablespoons of whole cumin seeds in a skillet and toast for a few minutes over medium heat, shaking the pan every now and then, until the cumin is fragrant and beginning to turn a golden brown color. Dump it into a spice grinder or clean coffee grinder and grind to a powder. Store it in a jar with a tight-fitting lid; it will last a couple of months.

Farmstand Salsa

25 minutes | Makes about 4 cups

I came up with this recipe after a trip to a farmstand last summer. The fresh, raw corn is really sweet and tastes great with chips.

Kernels from 2 ears of fresh sweet corn

$\frac{1}{2}$ medium red onion, diced

2 green onions, white and green parts, chopped

1 $\frac{1}{2}$ pints cherry tomatoes, halved

1 avocado, halved, pitted, peeled, and chunked

1 jalapeño, sliced

$\frac{1}{4}$ bunch of fresh cilantro, chopped

Juice of 1 lemon

$\frac{1}{4}$ cup extra-virgin olive oil

Kosher salt and freshly ground black pepper

Put all the ingredients into a large mixing bowl, and gently toss them together. Season with salt and pepper.

ONE GREAT THING ABOUT
LIVING IN NEW YORK CITY
IS THAT AN HOUR OUTSIDE
OF TOWN IN ANY DIRECTION
YOU CAN FIND AMAZING
ORGANIC PRODUCE
AND FARMERS WHO TRULY **TAKE PRIDE IN THEIR CRAFT**

Mezze

I LOVE THE MEDITERRANEAN FLAVORS AND COMMUNAL SETTING OF WHAT THE GREEKS CALL MEZZE. AN INVITATION TO THIS LAZY, LATE-AFTERNOON MEAL USUALLY CONSISTS OF A SUNSET, OUZO, AND NOSHING THROUGH SOME OF THE GREATEST FLAVORS THE MEDITERRANEAN HAS TO OFFER: MARINATED olives, spicy chickpeas, crisp grilled sardines, stuffed vine leaves, eggplant with pistachios and mint, and crisp falafel. You can find variations on this tradition throughout the Mediterranean, from Greece to Morocco and even into Spain, in what the Spanish call *tapas*. The same flavors show up time and time again all throughout the region. The recipes in this section are easy to pull off; the only things you need are a sunset and an excuse to have people over.

Grilled Sardines

45 minutes | Serves 6

Grilled sardines are a Mediterranean staple. This recipe is from the sunny coast of Nice.

**1 pound fresh, whole sardines
(1 to 2 ounces each)**
Extra-virgin olive oil
**Kosher salt and freshly ground
black pepper**
**1 recipe Grapefruit, Tarragon, and
Green Olive Sauce (page 22)**

To clean the sardines, pull off the gills and then pull out the innards. Rinse the sardines well under cold water, rubbing to remove the scales. Pat them dry on paper towels.

Put a large grill pan on two burners over medium-high heat or preheat an outdoor gas or charcoal grill and get it very hot. Take a few paper towels and fold them several times to make a thick square. Blot a small amount of oil on the paper towels, then carefully and quickly wipe the hot grates of the grill to make a nonstick grilling surface.

Toss the sardines in olive oil to coat, and sprinkle with salt and pepper. Grill, turning, until cooked through, 2 to 3 minutes on each side. Serve with the chopped-herb sauce.

Smoky Grilled Eggplant

30 minutes | Makes about 2 cups

You can cook the eggplants on a grill or roast them in the oven at high temperature. Either way, the eggplant starts to char and melt, and then it gets very creamy. Grilling gives the eggplant a smoky flavor that adds a fantastic depth of flavor to the finished dish.

Put a large grill pan on two burners over medium-high heat or preheat an outdoor gas or charcoal grill and get it very hot. Take a few paper towels and fold them several times to make a thick square. Blot a small amount of oil on the paper towels. Then carefully and quickly wipe the hot grates of the grill to make a nonstick grilling surface. Pierce the eggplants in a few places with a fork, so the steam has somewhere to go when you cook them. Then grill the eggplants, turning them often, for about 10 minutes, until the skins are wrinkled and black and the eggplants are shriveled and soft. (You can also roast the eggplants in a 400°F. oven for 30 minutes.) Remove them from the grill or oven and let them stand until they've cooled off enough to handle. Then split the eggplants open and scoop out the flesh, getting rid of the skin and as many seeds as possible.

In a food processor, combine the garlic, tahini, lemon juice, and parsley and purée until smooth. Add the eggplant and season with cumin, salt, and pepper. Pulse several times to make a thick, coarse purée. Pour in the oil and pulse again to blend. Taste for salt and pepper. Pour into a serving bowl and garnish with mint leaves and chopped pistachios. Drizzle with a little olive oil, too. Serve with pita wedges for dipping.

2 medium eggplants (about 1 pound total)
4 garlic cloves, coarsely chopped
1/4 cup tahini (sesame seed paste)
Juice of 1 lemon
1 handful of fresh flat-leaf parsley, coarsely chopped
1/2 teaspoon ground cumin (toasted, if you have it; see Note, page 96)
Kosher salt and freshly ground black pepper
1/2 cup extra-virgin olive oil
Fresh mint leaves, for garnish
2 tablespoons chopped toasted pistachios
Pita bread cut into wedges, for dipping

Falafel with Tahini Sauce

1 hour + an overnight soaking | Serves 4

It's hard to believe that a recipe this good is so simple. Dried chickpeas are soaked in water, then ground to make a kind of starchy milk that holds the batter together. When the falafel are deep-fried, the raw chickpeas swell and get fluffy like a soft bread. The falafel are crisp on the outside and have a delicious, savory flavor.

2 cups dried chickpeas, picked
through and rinsed

1 teaspoon baking powder

1 small onion, coarsely chopped

2 garlic cloves, smashed

1 tablespoon cumin seeds, toasted
and ground (see Note, page 96)

1 tablespoon coriander seeds, toasted
and ground

$\frac{1}{4}$ teaspoon dried red pepper flakes

2 handfuls of fresh flat-leaf parsley,
coarsely chopped

1 handful of fresh cilantro, coarsely
chopped

Kosher salt and freshly ground
black pepper

Vegetable oil, for frying

8 warm pita breads, cut in halves

Tahini Sauce (recipe follows)

Shredded lettuce

Sliced tomatoes

Chopped cucumbers

Put the dried chickpeas in a large bowl and add cool water to cover by 2 inches. Soak in the refrigerator for at least 12 hours or up to 48; the chickpeas will swell to triple their original size. Drain and rinse thoroughly.

Put the soaked chickpeas, baking powder, onion, garlic, spices, and herbs in the bowl of a food processor and pulse to coarsely grind. The mixture shouldn't be entirely smooth, but you don't want any whole chickpeas in the mix, either. Scrape down the sides of the bowl as you need to. Taste and season generously with salt and pepper. Transfer to a bowl and refrigerate while you heat the oil; that should take about 15 minutes.

Heat 3 inches of the oil in a deep-fryer or deep, heavy pot to 375°F. on a frying thermometer. Roll the falafel mixture into balls the size of Ping-Pong balls. (You can also use an ice-cream scoop.) Carefully slip a few at a time into the hot oil, making sure they don't stick to the bottom. Fry until the falafels are a crusty dark brown all over, about 5 minutes per batch, turning several times as they cook. Remove the falafels with a slotted spoon and drain on a platter lined with paper towels.

Open the pita bread halves to make pockets (don't split all the way) and put 3 fried falafels into each. Drizzle with the tahini sauce and layer with lettuce, tomatoes, and cucumbers. Serve immediately.

Tahini Sauce   Makes about 1 cup

$\frac{1}{2}$ cup tahini (sesame seed paste) | $\frac{1}{2}$ cup plain yogurt or water
| Juice of 1 lemon | Pinch of kosher salt | Pinch of paprika

Combine all the ingredients in a bowl and mix well with a whisk until smooth and creamy. Taste for salt, paprika, and lemon.

Tabbouleh

45 minutes + resting time | Serves 4 to 6

When made well, tabbouleh can be very satisfying on a hot day. All of the vegetables are crisp and cold and wrapped up with the bright flavors of olive oil and lemon juice. Perfect with a grilled piece of fish.

1 cup bulgur wheat (fine to medium grind)

2 cups warm water

1 pound ripe tomatoes, seeded and chopped (about 2 cups)

1 bunch of green onions, white and green parts, chopped (about 1 cup)

1 hothouse cucumber, halved, seeded, and diced (about 2 cups)

2 large bunches of fresh flat-leaf parsley, chopped (about 2 cups)

1 bunch of fresh mint leaves, chopped (about $1/2$ cup)

$1/4$ cup extra-virgin olive oil

Juice of 2 lemons

$1/2$ teaspoon ground cumin (toasted, if you have it; see Note, page 96)

Kosher salt and freshly ground black pepper

Put the bulgur in a large bowl and pour in the water. Cover with a plate or plastic wrap and let stand for 30 to 45 minutes to hydrate and soften. Drain in a strainer, pressing with the back of a wooden spoon to squeeze out as much water as possible.

Put the tomatoes, green onions, cucumber, parsley, and mint into another bowl. Add the olive oil, lemon juice, and cumin, and give it a stir. Season with salt and pepper. Add the bulgur and toss to coat with the seasonings. Let the tabbouleh sit for a few hours to allow the flavors to penetrate the wheat. Serve at room temperature.

Chickpeas Marinated in Olive Oil, Whole Cumin, and Chile

1 ¹/₂ hours + overnight soaking | Serves 8

I picked up this recipe at a restaurant in Valencia on the coast of Spain. I had ordered the chickpeas to tide me over while waiting for my dinner to arrive. They were creamy and spicy and went really well with the wine. They were served with toothpicks so you had to sort of spearfish the chickpeas, one by one, out of the bowl. In Spain they eat so late—I was famished and ate three bowls.

Soak the chickpeas overnight in cold water to cover. Drain. Put the chickpeas and bay leaves in a large pot. Cover with cold water and put the pot over medium heat. Bring to a boil, reduce the heat, and simmer until the chickpeas are tender, about 1 hour and 20 minutes. About halfway through the cooking, season with salt and pepper. This gives the chickpeas time to soften so that the seasoning can penetrate. Check the water periodically and add more if necessary to keep the peas covered. Drain the chickpeas, discard the bay leaves, and transfer to a serving bowl. Add the remaining ingredients and toss well. Season generously with salt and pepper and taste for lemon. Hit it with a drizzle of olive oil before serving.

1 pound dried chickpeas, picked through and rinsed

2 bay leaves

Kosher salt and freshly ground black pepper

¹/₂ cup extra-virgin olive oil, plus extra for drizzling

Juice of 1 lemon

2 teaspoons whole cumin seeds, toasted (not ground)

1 tablespoon paprika

1 fresh Thai bird chile or other hot green chile, chopped

CONSUMING

This chapter is all about those nights when the take-out menus are looking **PRETTY TEMPTING**. Trust me, though, cooking doesn't have to be too complicated or consume too much of your time. The dishes in this chapter are designed with **PRACTICALITY IN MIND**. They can be banged out with just a quick trip to the market, any night of the week. They're **IMPRESSIVE MEALS** that you'll be proud to make—and you can keep that tip in your pocket.

Spicy Chicken Broth with Tortillas, Avocado, and Lime

45 minutes | Serves 4

In a little town called Isla Mujeres on the Yucatan peninsula in Mexico, I stayed at a rustic place with just a hut and a hammock. Every night the lady who owned the place cooked for me. She made this soup one night. It is so good, so delicious—super-clean flavor. Just chicken broth spiced with jalapeño, chunks of chicken, and avocado. The broth is spicy, the avocado is creamy, and there's a big squeeze of lime at the end—it's a roller-coaster of flavors in a bowl.

Put a stockpot over medium heat and coat with a 2-count of olive oil. Add the onions, garlic, tomatoes, and jalapeños and cook for 15 minutes, or until the vegetables get pulpy. Pour in the stock, season with salt and pepper, and simmer for 20 to 25 minutes.

Meanwhile, heat 1 inch of canola oil in a skillet over medium-high heat. When the oil begins to smoke, add the tortilla strips in batches and fry until they are crisp on all sides. Remove with a slotted spoon to a paper-towel–lined platter and sprinkle with salt while they are still hot.

Divide the shredded chicken among 4 soup bowls. Ladle the hot soup over the meat. Top with the diced avocado and fried tortilla strips. Garnish with cilantro and lime wedges.

Extra-virgin olive oil

2 medium onions, diced

3 garlic cloves, minced

3 medium-size ripe tomatoes, chopped

2 jalapeños, minced

1 quart chicken stock, homemade (see page 36) or store-bought

Kosher salt and freshly ground black pepper

Canola oil, for frying

4 corn tortillas, cut into $1/8$-inch-wide strips

1 $1/2$ cups shredded cooked chicken (see page 37)

3 avocados, halved, pitted, peeled, and diced

$1/2$ cup coarsely chopped fresh cilantro

1 lime, cut in wedges

Baby Eggplant with Curry and Coconut Milk
45 minutes | Serves 4

The cooking styles of India vary from one region to another at least as much as the food of Mediterranean France is different from the flavors of Alsace. This dish represents the sunny flavors of southern India, where coconut is often used in curries. In this recipe, you can taste the extent to which southern Indian cuisine pulls from the same ingredient shelf as Thai food.

Heat ¼ cup of the ghee in a large pot over medium heat. Add the onion and sprinkle with the curry powder. Cook and stir for 3 to 5 minutes, until the onion is soft. Add the cashews, shredded coconut, coconut milk, and vegetable broth. Bring up to a simmer and cook gently for 15 to 20 minutes.

In the meantime, cut the eggplants into chunks. Heat the remaining ¼ cup of ghee in a deep skillet or Dutch oven over medium-high heat. When you see a slight smoke, add the eggplant and cook, stirring, until it gets charred and sticky, about 3 minutes.

When the coconut sauce is cooked, purée with a hand-held blender until it's pretty smooth. Pour the sauce over the eggplant and toss in the cinnamon stick and chile. Season with salt and simmer for 15 minutes, or until thick. Give a squeeze of lemon to brighten the flavor, garnish with mint leaves, and serve with steamed basmati rice and/or flatbread.

Ghee **Makes ¾ cup**

1 cup (2 sticks) unsalted butter

Put the butter in a heavy saucepan over medium heat and swirl the pot as it heats so that the butter melts slowly and does not sizzle or brown. Once it has melted, increase the heat and bring the butter to a boil. When the surface is covered with foam, stir gently and reduce the heat to the lowest possible setting. Gently simmer, uncovered and undisturbed, for 20 to 30 minutes, until the milk solids in the bottom of the pan have turned golden brown and the butter on top is transparent. Strain the ghee through a sieve lined with several layers of cheese-cloth. The ghee should be perfectly clear and smell nutty. Use immediately or pour into a glass jar, seal tightly, and refrigerate.

½ cup Ghee (see recipe below) or canola oil

1 onion, chopped

1 tablespoon curry powder, homemade (see page 28) or store-bought

1 cup unsalted raw or toasted cashews, coarsely chopped

½ cup shredded coconut (see Note, page 121)

2 cups coconut milk

2 cups vegetable broth

8 baby eggplants

1 cinnamon stick

1 dried red chile

Kosher salt

Juice of ½ lemon

Fresh mint leaves, for garnish

Stir-Fried Green Beans with Peanut Sauce, Fresh Tofu, and Chiles

45 minutes | Serves 4

This dish is like a Chinese McBLT: The hot side's hot, the cold side's cold. The green beans are hot and spicy, the tofu is cold and fresh, and you pile the stir-fried green beans on a plate and put the cold tofu on top. It's delicious after-work cooking at its finest. The vegetables are fresh, the peanut butter sauce is creamy and spicy, and the tofu is rich and full of protein.

$1/2$ **cup peanut oil**

1 $1/4$ **pounds green beans, halved on the bias**

1-inch piece of fresh ginger, peeled and minced

4 garlic cloves, minced

2 green onions, white and green parts, chopped

1 dried red chile

Kosher salt and freshly ground black pepper

$1/2$ **cup chicken stock, homemade (see page 36) or store-bought**

1 tablespoon cornstarch

2 tablespoons low-sodium soy sauce

1 tablespoon rice vinegar

1 tablespoon sugar

3 tablespoons creamy peanut butter

2 strips of orange zest

1 (15-ounce) block of firm tofu, cut into 1-inch cubes

1 fresh jalapeño pepper, sliced crosswise into rounds

$1/4$ **cup roasted peanuts, chopped**

Handful of fresh cilantro leaves

Pour the peanut oil in a wok and place over high heat. When the oil is smoking hot, add the beans and stir-fry for 2 minutes; remove to a platter lined with paper towels to drain. Very carefully, drain all but 2 tablespoons of the hot oil into a heat-proof container.

Add the ginger, garlic, green onions, and chile to the oil remaining in the wok and stir-fry until you can smell the fragrance of the aromatics. Return the green beans to the wok and season with salt and pepper. In a small bowl, stir the chicken stock with the cornstarch to make a slurry and add that to the wok. Add the soy sauce, vinegar, sugar, peanut butter, and orange zest. Simmer until the sauce is thickened and the beans are tender, 5 to 7 minutes. Garnish with the tofu, sliced jalapeño, chopped peanuts, and cilantro and serve with steamed rice.

Martin Yan's Szechuan Eggplant

45 minutes | Serves 4

One of the most talented cooks and funniest people I've ever bumped into is the legendary Martin Yan. He helped open the door for food television twenty years ago and he's never looked back. He has published many cookbooks and his television shows are broadcast throughout the world. He lives in San Francisco; if you ever get a chance to walk around Chinatown with him, he's a rock star.

Yan's food is classic, intelligent, and authentic, like the man himself. To taste his food is to truly understand Asian flavors. He made this recipe for me for lunch one day; it is a good example of how simple great Chinese food can be.

Cut the eggplants in half lengthwise and then slice crosswise into wedges, each no more than 1 inch wide.

Heat a 14-inch wok or large skillet over medium-high heat and add the peanut and sesame oils. Tilt the pan to coat all sides. When you see a slight smoke, add a layer of eggplant and stir-fry until seared and sticky, about 3 minutes. Season with salt and pepper. Remove the eggplant to a platter and cook the remaining eggplant in the same way, adding more oil as needed.

When all the eggplant is out of the pan, add the green onions, ginger, garlic, and chile and stir-fry for a minute until fragrant. Add the stock and bring to a boil. While that heats, in a small bowl stir together the soy sauce, vinegar, sugar, and cornstarch to dissolve the sugar and cornstarch. Pour the soy-sauce mixture into the wok and cook for another minute, or until the sauce has thickened. Return the eggplant to the pan and toss until the sauce is absorbed. Garnish with sesame seeds, basil, and cilantro and serve hot.

5 Asian eggplants (about 2 pounds total)

3 tablespoons peanut oil

1 tablespoon toasted sesame oil

Kosher salt and freshly ground black pepper

2 green onions, white and green parts, sliced on a diagonal into 2-inch pieces

1-inch piece of fresh ginger, peeled and minced

3 garlic cloves, minced

1 fresh hot red chile, sliced

3/4 cup chicken stock, homemade (see page 36) or store-bought

3 tablespoons low-sodium soy sauce

1 tablespoon rice vinegar

1 tablespoon light brown sugar

1 tablespoon cornstarch

1 tablespoon toasted sesame seeds, for garnish

Chopped fresh basil (Thai holy, or regular), for garnish

Chopped fresh cilantro, for garnish

Curried Cauliflower with Chickpeas and Tomatoes

40 minutes | Serves 4

This recipe uses one of the fresh-milled spice mixtures—homemade curry powder—in the front of the book. Everything happens in one pot. This is a good, fast vegetarian meal—light and full of flavor—and a beautiful way to experience the taste of India.

¼ cup Ghee (page 111) or canola oil

1 onion, finely chopped

2 tablespoons curry powder, homemade (see page 28) or store-bought

1-inch piece of fresh ginger, peeled and julienned

2 ripe tomatoes, chopped

2 tablespoons tomato paste

1 head of cauliflower (about 1 pound), cut into florets

3 cups canned chickpeas, drained and rinsed

Kosher salt

Fresh cilantro leaves, for garnish

Heat the ghee in a deep skillet or pot over medium heat. Add the onion, curry powder, and ginger and cook, stirring, for a few minutes to soften the onion. Then add the tomatoes and cook, stirring, until the tomatoes break down and soften, about 6 minutes. Stir in the tomato paste and 1 cup of water to dissolve the paste. Gently fold in the cauliflower and chickpeas. Reduce the heat to medium-low, cover, and simmer until the cauliflower is tender, 15 to 20 minutes. Uncover and continue cooking until the sauce has thickened and the cauliflower and chickpeas are coated with a thick gravy. Season with salt and garnish with cilantro before serving.

Saag Paneer

45 minutes | Serves 4

Translated, saag paneer means spinach with cheese. Paneer is a fresh, large-curd Indian cheese, similar to ricotta but drier. Some traditional recipes for paneer use water buffalo milk, the same milk used in Italy to make mozzarella cheese. It's very rich. If you can't find paneer, firm tofu is a great substitute. Either way, this is great, healthy midweek cooking—it's a plateful of flavor.

2 pounds fresh baby spinach,
**   stems trimmed**
¹/₄ cup Ghee (page 111)
**   or canola oil**
¹/₂ pound cubed paneer cheese
2 onions, finely chopped
3 garlic cloves, minced
1 teaspoon grated fresh ginger
1 teaspoon curry powder,
**   homemade (see page 28) or**
**   store-bought**
¹/₂ cup buttermilk
¹/₄ cup plain yogurt
Kosher salt

Bring a large pot of water to a boil, toss in the spinach, and blanch for 1 minute, or until very tender. Dump the spinach into a colander and press firmly with the back of a spoon to extract as much water as possible. Roughly chop, then set aside.

Heat the ghee in a deep skillet over medium-high heat. Add the cubed paneer and fry for a couple of minutes until light brown on all sides, turning gently to avoid breaking up the cubes. Remove the cheese from the skillet and set aside.

Return the skillet to the heat, add the onions, garlic, and ginger, and sauté, stirring, for about 5 minutes, or until soft. Sprinkle the mixture with the curry powder and continue to cook, stirring, to marry the flavors, about 1 minute. Fold in the chopped spinach and give everything a good toss. Shut off the heat and stir in the buttermilk and yogurt. The mixture should be creamy and somewhat thick. Gently fold in the fried paneer cubes, season with salt, and serve with steamed basmati rice and/or flatbread.

Sesame Chicken

45 minutes | Serves 4

The all-time take-out classic. After the chicken is marinated with egg whites, it is quickly deep fried so it gets a nice deep crunch. The sauce has a rich sweet and sour flavor. This smells and tastes like delicious Chinese cooking.

In a large bowl, beat the egg whites with the cornstarch. Add the sesame oil, soy sauce, and rice vinegar and stir. Add the chicken and marinate in the fridge for 30 minutes to 1 hour.

Bring a large saucepan of salted water to a boil for the broccoli.

Pour the oil into a wok and heat it to 370°F. to 375°F. on a deep-fry thermometer. Meanwhile, season the flour on a plate with a good amount of salt and pepper and mix with your fingers to incorporate the seasoning. Working in batches, remove the chicken from the marinade, dredge it in the flour, and deep-fry until crisp and lightly browned, about 1 minute. Remove from the oil with a slotted spoon, and transfer to a paper-towel–lined platter. Pour the oil out into a heat-proof container to reuse or discard.

Now drop your broccoli into the boiling salted water. Return the water to a boil and cook the broccoli for just 1 minute, or until it's crisp-tender and a bright green color. Drain.

Meanwhile, you need to make the sauce, so combine the ketchup, orange juice, soy sauce, honey, vinegar, fresh chile, ginger, and chile paste in the wok and put it back over medium heat. Add 1 tablespoon of water to thin and stir it all together over the heat until it's warmed through.

Put the broccoli on a serving platter. Fold the chicken into the hot sauce until it's well coated and spoon it onto the bed of broccoli. Sprinkle with sesame seeds and serve.

2 large egg whites

2 tablespoons cornstarch

1 tablespoon toasted sesame oil

1 teaspoon low-sodium soy sauce

1 teaspoon rice vinegar

8 boneless, skinless chicken thighs, cut into thin strips

1 quart peanut oil, for deep-frying

2 to 2¹/₂ cups all-purpose flour, for dredging

Kosher salt and freshly ground black pepper

1 bunch of broccoli, trimmed and cut into florets

SAUCE

²/₃ cup ketchup

¹/₂ cup fresh orange juice

¹/₄ cup low-sodium soy sauce

2 tablespoons honey

2 tablespoons rice vinegar

1 fresh hot green chile, chopped

1¹/₂ tablespoons minced fresh ginger

2 teaspoons chile paste, such as sambal

2 tablespoons toasted sesame seeds, for garnish

IN CERTAIN PARTS OF MY
NEIGHBORHOOD IN CHINATOWN IF YOU
DIDN'T NOTICE THE EMPIRE STATE
BUILDING OVER YOUR SHOULDER,
YOU'D SWEAR
YOU'RE IN BEIJING.

Wonton of Salmon with Green Curry and Coconut

1 hour | Makes 50 wontons

FILLING

1 pound wild salmon fillet, skin and
    pin bones removed, minced
2 tablespoons minced fresh ginger
2 tablespoons minced fresh cilantro
2 tablespoons minced shallots
2 teaspoons rice vinegar
1 tablespoon toasted sesame oil
1 large egg white
Kosher salt and freshly ground
    black pepper

SAUCE

2 tablespoons vegetable oil
2 teaspoons minced garlic
1 teaspoon minced fresh ginger
1 small hot red chile, split
1 teaspoon green curry paste
    (see Note)
1 (14.5-ounce) can unsweetened
    coconut milk
1 lemongrass stalk, bottom 3 inches
    only, split and pounded
Juice of 2 limes

1 (1-pound) package of 3¹/₂-inch
    round wonton wrappers
1 egg white, lightly beaten
Cornstarch, for dusting
Small handful of shredded coconut
    (see Note)
Fresh basil leaves (Thai holy or
    regular), for garnish
Fresh mint leaves, for garnish

When I moved to Chinatown from Brooklyn a few years ago, one of the joys of the neighborhood was a local wonton shop. For me, mastering the art of the simple Chinese dumpling became a prerequisite to living in the neighborhood—if you live in Chinatown, I thought, you *have* to know how to make a wonton. Be sure to read the instructions below twice before starting, but once you've got the hang of it, it's as simple as folding a shirt (a stuffed shirt, that is).

First thing you're going to do is make the filling. In a large mixing bowl, combine the salmon, ginger, cilantro, shallots, vinegar, sesame oil, and egg white. Stir well and season with salt and pepper. (You may refrigerate this for several hours if you're not ready to cook.)

Next, get going on the sauce. In a large sauté pan, heat the oil over medium heat. Add the garlic, ginger, and chile and cook for 2 minutes. Add the green curry paste and stir well to combine. Pour in the coconut milk and toss in the lemongrass. Bring to a low boil. Stir in the lime juice and taste for salt and pepper. Fish out the lemongrass and chile and discard. Take the sauce off the heat and bring a big pot of lightly salted water to a low boil while you fill the wontons.

Lay a wonton wrapper on a flat surface and brush with the beaten egg white. Place a teaspoon of the filling in the center. Bring the sides up to meet over the top of the filling to make a half-moon shape. Crimp the edges to seal. Repeat with the remaining wrappers and filling. Lightly dust the filled wontons with cornstarch to keep them from sticking together and place them on a cookie sheet.

Put the coconut in a small sauté pan and toast over medium heat until lightly browned and fragrant. Set that aside.

When all of the wontons have been filled, carefully drop them 8 to 10 at a time into the boiling water and cook for 3 minutes, no more. Drain in a colander, then transfer to a serving bowl. Rewarm the sauce

over low heat and pour over the wontons; toss carefully. Sprinkle the toasted coconut over the wontons, toss in some basil and mint leaves, and serve.

NOTE | You'll find green curry paste in Asian markets and some health-food stores. You can use either the unsweetened, dried coconut that's sold at health-food stores (it's labeled *desiccated*) or Indian grocers, or the sweetened, flaked coconut that's sold at any supermarket.

Lemon Chicken with White Wine and Parsley

30 minutes | Serves 4

The lemons are sliced paper-thin and melt into jam, which gives the sauce a great flavor at the end.

4 skinless, boneless chicken breasts
  (about 1 $^1/_2$ pounds total)

1 cup all-purpose flour, for dredging

Kosher salt and freshly ground
  black pepper

4 large eggs

$^1/_4$ cup extra-virgin olive oil

$^1/_2$ lemon, thinly sliced into rounds

$^1/_2$ cup dry white wine, such as
  Pinot Grigio

1 cup chicken stock, homemade
  (see page 36) or store-bought

Juice of $^1/_2$ lemon

2 tablespoons unsalted butter

$^1/_4$ cup chopped fresh flat-leaf parsley

Preheat the oven to 200°F.

Put the chicken breasts side by side on a cutting board and lay a piece of plastic wrap over them. Pound the chicken breasts with a flat meat mallet or the bottom of a heavy saucepan to about $^1/_4$ inch thick. Put the flour in a shallow platter and season with a fair amount of salt and pepper. Mix with a fork to distribute the seasoning. In a wide bowl, beat the eggs with 3 tablespoons of water to make an egg wash.

Put the oil into a large skillet and heat over medium-high heat until nice and hot. Dredge the chicken in the seasoned flour, and pat off the excess. Dip the chicken in the egg wash to coat completely, letting the excess drip off. Add the cutlets to the hot oil and fry for 2 minutes on each side, or until golden, turning once. Remove the cutlets to a large platter (in a single layer) and put in the oven to keep warm.

Now toss the lemon slices into the pan and cook for a minute or two, until fragrant. Add the wine, stock, and lemon juice, and simmer for 5 minutes to reduce the sauce slightly. Roll the pat of butter in the seasoned flour and add it to the skillet. This will help to thicken the sauce. Stir or whisk to emulsify and dissolve the flour. Reduce the heat to medium-low and return the chicken to the pan. Fish out the lemon slices with tongs and put them on top of the cutlets. Simmer the whole thing gently for about 2 minutes to heat the chicken through. Season with salt and pepper and garnish with chopped parsley before serving.

Roasted Chicken Stuffed with Lemon and Herbs

A little under 2 hours | Serves 6

You can judge a good cook on the basis of one thing alone, and that is, can he or she make a perfect chicken or not. It's funny how a lot of recipes make this simple process so difficult. The keys to roasting chicken are flavor, temperature, and time. You've got to season the chicken well, inside and out, so that the flavors really permeate the meat. Lemon makes the meat taste bright, and garlic and rosemary give it deep flavor. The perfect temperature to get a really crispy skin while the meat cooks through is 400°F. I guarantee you, roasted this way, your bird will really taste like something.

Preheat the oven to 400°F.

Rinse the chicken inside and out with cool water, then pat it dry with paper towels. Season the cavity with salt and pepper, and stuff it with the lemon, garlic, and herbs. Place the chicken, breast side up, in a roasting pan. Tie the legs of the chicken together with kitchen twine to help hold its shape. Toss the potatoes around the chicken. Season the whole thing with a fair amount of salt and pepper and drizzle with the olive oil.

Roast the chicken and potatoes for 1 to 1½ hours. Don't forget to baste the chicken with the drippings and rotate the pan every 20 minutes or so to get the skin golden and crispy. The chicken is done when an instant-read thermometer says 165°F. when inserted into the thickest part of the thigh (the legs of the chicken should wiggle easily from the sockets, too). Remove the chicken to a platter and let stand for 10 minutes, so the juices settle back into the meat before carving. Serve with the roasted potatoes on the side.

1 free-range chicken (4 to 5 pounds)
Kosher salt and freshly ground black pepper
1 lemon, halved
1 head of garlic, halved horizontally
¼ bunch of fresh rosemary
¼ bunch of fresh thyme
¼ bunch of fresh flat-leaf parsley
1½ pounds red new potatoes, left whole, if small, or halved, if large
¼ cup extra-virgin olive oil

Pan-Roasted Chicken with Mushrooms, Shallots, and Rosemary

45 minutes | Serves 4

This is a great way to cook a whole chicken and shows off a method that I love to use, called "pan-roasting." Pan-roasting is a great method because you start the chicken on the stovetop to get the skin crisp, and then just put the whole pan in the oven and let the oven do the hard part. Using a quartered rather than a whole chicken saves cooking time.

Preheat the oven to 350°F.

Season the chicken on both sides with a generous amount of salt and pepper. Put 2 large cast-iron or regular ovenproof skillets on the stove over medium heat and get them good and hot. Drizzle each pan with a 2-count of oil and lay the chicken in the hot fat, $\frac{1}{2}$ chicken per pan, skin side down. Cook for about 5 minutes, or until the skin begins to set and crisp. Divide the mushrooms, shallots, and rosemary between the pans. Stick both pans in the hot oven and roast for about 30 minutes, or until the chicken is cooked and the mushrooms and shallots are soft and roasted.

Take the pans out of the oven. To finish up, you want to make a quick sauce using the flavors left in the bottoms of the skillets. Take all the stuff out of the pans and arrange on 4 dinner plates or a platter to keep warm while you're preparing the pan sauce. Pour out all but 1 tablespoon of the rendered chicken fat in each pan (if there is that much) and return the skillets to the stovetop. (If you have got a lot of juices, boil the juices down until all you have left is fat and pan drippings; then pour off all but 1 tablespoon of the fat, if there is that much.) Stir $\frac{1}{2}$ cup water and the juice of $\frac{1}{2}$ lemon into each pan and cook over medium heat, scraping up the flavors with a wooden spoon. Cook the liquid down to a syrup, 3 to 5 minutes. Drizzle the pan sauce over the chicken and vegetables, season with salt and pepper, and serve immediately.

1 chicken (about 3 pounds), quartered

Kosher salt and freshly ground black pepper

$\frac{1}{4}$ cup extra-virgin olive oil

20 fresh white mushrooms, halved

8 medium shallots, unpeeled, split in half

4 fresh rosemary sprigs

1 cup water

Juice of 1 lemon

FLORENCE PRIME MEAT MA

THERE ARE ONLY A FEW OLD-WORLD BUTCHER SHOPS LEFT IN NEW YORK CITY, AND THIS IS ONE OF MY FAVORITES. THEY DRY-AGE THEIR BEEF FOR TWO WEEKS, AND IT'S AMONG THE BEST I'VE EVER TASTED.

Steak Frites

1 ¹/₂ hours | Serves 4

The secret to perfect French fries is the double cooking. First you blanch them in oil at a low temperature to cook them all the way through and then you fry them a second time at a higher temperature just to crisp and brown them. Wrap the fries in parchment-paper cones and stick them in the bottom of mini martini shakers for serving individually.

4 New York strip steaks, about 10 ounces each

Extra-virgin olive oil

Kosher salt and coarsely ground black pepper

1 handful of fresh thyme sprigs

1 handful of fresh rosemary sprigs

2 shallots, finely chopped

¹/₂ cup Cognac or brandy

¹/₂ cup demi-glace (store-bought is fine) or reduced veal stock (see page 38)

¹/₄ cup heavy cream

1 tablespoon Dijon mustard

2 tablespoons green peppercorns, drained

1 bunch of watercress, stems trimmed

¹/₄ cup chopped fresh flat-leaf parsley

Rub both sides of the steaks with oil and season with a generous amount of salt and pepper. Place the steaks on a platter and spread the thyme and rosemary on top. Drizzle with a bit more olive oil and cover with plastic. Marinate in the fridge for at least 30 minutes, or up to an hour.

Put two large skillets over medium-high heat, drizzle each with a 2-count of olive oil, and heat until the oil is smoking. Brush the herbs off the steaks so that they don't burn. Put 2 steaks in each pan and cook for 5 to 7 minutes per side for medium-rare. Remove the steaks to a platter.

Pour off all but a few teaspoons of fat from the pans and put them back on the stove over medium-high heat. Divide the shallots between the pans and sauté, stirring with a spoon to scrape up the flavors in the bottom. Take the pans off the heat and pour ¹/₄ cup of the Cognac (premeasure—never pour directly from the bottle or you might have a fire) into each. Put the pans back on the stove and tilt the edges of the pans slightly over the burners to ignite the alcohol (or light with a kitchen lighter). The Cognac will flame for a few seconds then go out as the alcohol burns off. Scrape the contents of one of the pans into the other. Stir in the demi-glace and cream, and simmer for about 1 minute to thicken the sauce so it coats a spoon. Finish the sauce by stirring in the mustard and peppercorns. Taste and season with salt, if necessary.

To serve, arrange a fistful of watercress sprigs on each plate and put a steak on top of each. Drizzle the sauce over the steaks and garnish with chopped parsley. Serve with Pommes Frites.

Pommes Frites with Parsley Butter
Serves 4

4 medium Idaho potatoes, peeled | **1 quart peanut or vegetable oil**
| **Kosher salt** | **¼ cup (½ stick) unsalted butter, cut in chunks** |
2 tablespoons chopped fresh flat-leaf parsley | **1 garlic clove, minced**

To blanch the fries, peel the potatoes and cut them into uniform ¼-inch sticks. Use a knife, mandoline, or French-fry cutter to do this—whatever's easiest. Put the fries in a bowl, put the bowl in the sink, and run cold water over them. You'll see that the water is cloudy from potato starch. Let the water run until it's clear; getting rid of the starch in this way will make the fries crisp. Dry the potato sticks thoroughly on kitchen towels to keep the hot oil from splattering.

Pour the oil into a deep-fryer or heavy saucepan so that it reaches halfway up the sides and heat it to 325°F. on a deep-fry thermometer. Working in batches (so the pot isn't crowded and the oil temperature does not plummet), cook the fries for 3 minutes, until soft but not browned. Remove with a long-handled metal strainer and drain on brown paper bags, if you have any; bags work great for this because they're very absorbent.

Increase the oil temperature to 375°F. Still working in batches, return the blanched potatoes to the oil and cook a second time for 2 minutes, or until golden and crispy. Drain on fresh brown paper bags, then put them in a serving bowl. Salt the fries while they're still hot.

Combine the butter, parsley, and garlic in a saucepan over medium heat and swirl the pan around until the butter is completely melted. Pour this seasoned butter over the fries and toss gently. Serve with the steak.

Steamed Black Bass in Miso Soup with Udon and Shiitakes

1 hour | Serves 2

I always make more of this Japanese soup stock (*dashi*) than I need at a time; the extra will hold in the refrigerator for up to a week or you can freeze it for several months. If you have got the dashi, you have got an instant base for future soups and stews. You'll also need a wok and a bamboo steamer for this recipe.

First make the Japanese soup stock, or dashi: In a 4-quart saucepan, combine 3 quarts of water, the kelp, and bonito flakes and place over medium-low heat. Allow the water to come slowly to a simmer. This should take about 10 minutes. Turn off the heat just as the stock reaches a boil. Let the stock sit for a minute or two and then strain out the solids. Pour 1 quart of the dashi into a wok; reserve the remaining 2 quarts for another use. Put the wok over medium heat. Whisk in the miso until smooth. Toss in the mushrooms and bring the stock to a simmer.

Lightly coat the bottom of a 12-inch bamboo steamer with nonstick cooking spray. Season both sides of the fish fillets with salt and pepper and lay them side by side in the steamer, skin side up. Cut the ginger lengthwise in strips and arrange it on top of the fish so the flavor can permeate the flesh. Sprinkle the cilantro over everything. Nestle the bok choy halves in the steamer, side by side. Cover with the bamboo lid, set the steamer inside the wok over the simmering stock, and steam for 15 to 20 minutes, until the fish is cooked. Carefully lift out the bamboo steamer and throw the udon noodles and green onions into the simmering stock. Cook for about a minute, or until the noodles are tender.

To serve, ladle the miso soup into 2 wide shallow bowls, scoop the noodles into the soup, and lay the bok choy and fish on top of that. Garnish with more cilantro, sprinkle lightly with the chili–sesame salt, and serve.

NOTE | Chile–sesame salt is available at Asian grocers.

3 (6-inch) pieces of dried kelp (*kombu*), wiped with a damp paper towel

1 ¹⁄₂ cups dried bonito flakes

2 tablespoons light miso

8 ounces shiitake mushrooms, stemmed, and halved

2 (6-ounce) center-cut black sea bass fillets, skin on

Kosher salt and freshly ground black pepper

2-inch piece of fresh ginger, peeled

1 handful of fresh cilantro, plus more for garnish

2 heads of baby bok choy, halved lengthwise

1 pound fresh udon noodles

2 green onions, white and green parts, chopped

Several shakes of chile–sesame salt (see Note)

Pan-Seared Tuna with Avocado
30 minutes I Serves 4

This is one of my favorite recipes in the book for the sauce alone. The combination of soy sauce, olive oil, and lime juice is mind-blowing. With a thick slab of tuna and creamy avocado, I couldn't be happier.

Extra-virgin olive oil

4 (6-ounce) blocks of sushi-quality tuna

Kosher salt and freshly ground black pepper

1 recipe Ginger-Soy Vinaigrette (page 32)

2 ripe avocados, halved, pitted, peeled, and sliced

Place a large skillet over medium-high heat and coat with a 2-count of olive oil. Season the tuna generously with salt and pepper. Lay the tuna in the hot oil and sear for 1 minute on each side to form a slight crust. Pour half of the vinaigrette into the pan to coat the fish. Remove the fish to plates and serve with the sliced avocado and the remaining vinaigrette drizzled over everything.

Roasted Salmon with Pickled Cucumbers and Dates
30 minutes I Serves 4

This whole dish can come together in about 20 minutes. The sweet cucumber pickles taste amazing and need only a little knife work; the dates are a sweet contrast to the chile and salmon.

2 hothouse cucumbers, thinly sliced

2 fresh hot red chiles, thinly sliced

2 large handfuls of fresh mint

$1/3$ cup dates, split lengthwise and pitted

2 cups rice vinegar

4 teaspoons sugar

Kosher salt and freshly ground black pepper

4 (6-ounce) center-cut salmon fillets, without skin

4 tablespoons sesame seeds

$1/4$ cup extra-virgin olive oil

In a mixing bowl, combine the cucumbers, chiles, mint, and dates. Pour in the vinegar and sprinkle with the sugar, salt, and pepper. Toss everything together so the cucumbers are well coated with the vinegar. The cucumbers will soften as they marinate and the flavors will deepen.

Preheat the oven to 350°F. Season both sides of the salmon with a fair amount of salt and pepper. Sprinkle the top of the salmon with the sesame seeds. Put a large cast-iron or other ovenproof skillet on the stove over medium heat. Coat the pan with the oil and when it is nice and hot, lay the salmon fillets in the pan, sesame-seed side down. Sear the salmon for 3 minutes, then put the skillet in the oven and roast the salmon for 10 minutes, or until it's just cooked through. (Do not turn the fish.) Serve the salmon on a pile of the pickled cucumbers.

Crisp Striped Bass with Zucchini

1 ¹/₂ hours | Serves 4

I came up with this recipe when I cooked at the Cannes film festival last year because the *courgettes* (as zucchini are called in France) looked just gorgeous at the market. I decided to incorporate a sort of grandma style: I sliced the lemon paper-thin, chopped some onion and fresh thyme, put it all together with the zucchini, and let it cook really slowly until this everyday vegetable was transformed into something that tasted truly amazing. The film festival was packed and this fish was a big hit.

ZUCCHINI

¹/₄ cup plus 2 tablespoons extra-
  virgin olive oil
1 lemon, preferably Meyer
1 small onion, finely minced
2 large zucchini, chopped into
  medium chunks
¹/₂ bunch of fresh thyme
1 bay leaf
Kosher salt and freshly ground
  black pepper

GREEN OLIVE BUTTER

2 tablespoons minced green olives
4 tablespoons unsalted butter
Kosher salt and freshly ground
  black pepper

BASS

Extra-virgin olive oil
4 (6-ounce) center-cut wild striped
  bass fillets (1 ¹/₂ pounds total),
  with skin
Kosher salt and freshly ground
  black pepper

Fried Zucchini Blossoms (page 44),
  for garnish

First make the zucchini. In a heavy-bottomed pot, heat ¹/₄ cup of the olive oil over medium-low heat. Thinly slice the lemon and add the onion and lemon slices and cook for 3 to 5 minutes, or until the onion is translucent. Add the zucchini to the pot and give it a stir. Add the thyme, bay leaf, and a generous amount of salt and pepper and stir well. Lower the heat, cover, and let the zucchini simmer very gently for 30 to 40 minutes, until it is soft and browned and the flavors are melded. Discard the bay leaf.

While that's going, make the olive butter. Let the butter soften at room temperature. Stir together the olives and butter until smooth. Season with salt and pepper. Cover and let that sit at room temperature.

When the zucchini is cooked, preheat the oven to 375°F. In a large ovenproof sauté pan, heat a 2-count of oil over medium heat until smoking. Put the fillets in the oil, skin side down, and sear for 2 to 3 minutes on one side only. The skin will start to seize and curl; use a spatula to press down on each fillet to flatten. When the skin is well seared, put the pan in the oven and cook until the fish is just cooked and still translucent in the center, about 10 minutes. (Cook the fish on one side only.)

To serve, divide the zucchini among 4 plates. Put the fish on top, skin side up, add a dollop of the green olive butter, and garnish with fried zucchini blossoms.

Pasta

THE ART OF MAKING FRESH PASTA IS AN OLD-WORLD CRAFT THAT I PICKED UP ON ONE OF MY TRIPS TO ITALY. IN BOLOGNA THERE'S A WORLD-FAMOUS PASTA SHOP CALLED LA STROGLINE. MARIA, THE OWNER, WON THE GOLDEN TORTELLINI AWARD THAT YEAR FOR THE BEST PASTA SHOP IN ITALY. WHEN YOU TOUCH FRESH pasta you truly understand that there's life beyond the box. As I watched Maria work, the process of mixing the semolina and eggs seemed effortless. Then she rolled out the dough—bright yellow from the yolks—in myriad shapes. The silky pasta, rich with olive oil, melted in my mouth.

FRESH PASTA'S KIND OF FUN TO MAKE;
IT'S AN INTERACTIVE THING TO DO WITH KIDS
WHO THINK SPAGHETTI COMES FROM A
SPAGHETTI TREE.

Fresh Pasta Dough

45 minutes | Makes about 1 pound

I always keep a box of good-quality dried pasta in my kitchen to use in a pinch, but I think once you master the truly simple art of making fresh pasta you may never go back. To make life easier, you can also freeze fresh pasta so you'll have it for the week. After you cut it into whatever shape you're using, portion it out into individual servings and put each portion in a sandwich bag. Store the bags in a plastic container in the freezer. When you're ready to cook, take the pasta from the freezer and throw it straight into the boiling water.

Fresh pasta's also kind of fun to make; it's an interactive thing to do with kids who think spaghetti comes from a spaghetti tree.

2 cups all-purpose flour, plus more for dusting

1 teaspoon kosher salt

3 large eggs

2 tablespoons extra-virgin olive oil

Put the flour on a clean, flat work surface. Add the salt and mix well. Shape that into a mound and then use the side of your hand to scoop out a well in the center. Add the 3 eggs and 1 tablespoon of the oil to the well and beat lightly with a fork. Gradually mix in the flour from the inside wall of the well, using a circular motion. Use one hand for mixing and the other to protect the outer wall. Continue to widen the well and incorporate the flour until the dough forms a ball. Knead and fold the dough until elastic and smooth; this should take about 10 minutes. Brush the surface with the remaining tablespoon of olive oil and wrap the dough in plastic wrap. Let it rest for about 30 minutes to allow the gluten to relax. The pasta is now ready to roll and cook.

Pappardelle Bolognese

2¹/₂ to 3 hours + 45 minutes if using fresh pasta | Serves 4 to 6

This is perfect Sunday-night comfort food, using very few ingredients. It's creamy and soft and really rich—satisfying, and with so much flavor.

In a large, heavy-bottomed saucepan, heat a 2-count of olive oil over medium heat. Add the onion, celery, carrots, and garlic and cook for about 10 minutes, stirring, until the vegetables are very tender but not browned.

Raise the heat a bit. Break the ground veal and beef into chunks and add them to the pan. Brown, breaking up the clumps with a wooden spoon, until the meat is no longer pink. Add the wine and simmer until evaporated. Then add the tomatoes and stock and season with salt and pepper. Lower the heat and simmer very slowly for 1¹/₂ to 2 hours, stirring now and then, until the sauce is very thick. Now add the milk—the milk will make the meat nice and tender—and simmer again until thickened, another 20 to 30 minutes. Taste again for salt and pepper. Mash the sauce against the side of the pan to really blend it. Transfer half of the sauce to a container and refrigerate for up to a week.

Bring a big pot of lightly salted water to a boil for the pasta.

If using fresh pasta, dust a baking sheet with cornmeal. Cut the pasta dough into big chunks. Cover and reserve the pieces you are not immediately using to prevent them from drying out. Dust the counter and dough with a little flour. Roll the chunk of dough through a pasta machine at the widest setting; you'll have a strip. Fold that strip in half, turn it 90 degrees, and roll it through again. Now you have a nice edge. Roll the dough another two or three times in the same direction, pulling and stretching it with the palm of your hand as it emerges from the rollers. Crank the setting down, and roll the dough through again, two or three times. Continue tightening and rolling, one setting at a time, until the machine is at the thinnest setting. Cut the sheet of dough lengthwise into wide (about 1-inch) strips, then put the noodles on the cornmeal-dusted baking sheet. Continue to roll and cut all of the pasta.

When you are ready to serve, drop the pasta into the boiling water and cook until al dente, 2 to 3 minutes for fresh pasta (8 or 9 minutes for dried). Drain and put the pasta into a big pasta bowl. Return the sauce remaining in the pot to a simmer and stir in the ricotta cheese. Pour the sauce over the drained pasta and give it a good toss. Garnish with oregano or basil, grated Parmigiano, and a drizzle of olive oil.

BOLOGNESE SAUCE

Extra-virgin olive oil
1 medium onion, finely chopped
2 celery stalks, finely chopped
2 carrots, peeled and finely chopped
5 garlic cloves, minced
1 pound ground veal
1 pound ground beef
1 cup dry white wine
2 (28-ounce) cans whole, peeled
   tomatoes, drained and crushed
   by hand
4 cups chicken stock, homemade
   (see page 36) or store-bought
Kosher salt and freshly ground
   black pepper
1 cup milk

1 recipe Fresh Pasta Dough (page
   140) or 1 pound dried tagliatelle
Cornmeal, for dusting
All-purpose flour, for rolling
1 large spoonful of ricotta cheese
1 handful of fresh oregano sprigs or
   basil leaves, torn into small pieces
1 handful of freshly grated
   Parmigiano-Reggiano, plus more
   for serving

Fettuccine with Porcinis and Walnuts

45 minutes + 45 minutes if using fresh pasta | Serves 4

This dish is straight from the hills of Tuscany. After you try this recipe, dried porcinis, easy to find in most grocery stores, will be a staple in your pantry, too.

4-ounce package dried porcini mushrooms

Extra-virgin olive oil

1 pound fresh porcini mushrooms, or whatever interesting mushrooms you can find in your supermarket, wiped clean and roughly chopped

2 garlic cloves, chopped

1 celery stalk, minced

2 tablespoons fresh sage, finely chopped

Kosher salt and freshly ground black pepper

$1/2$ cup freshly grated Pecorino cheese

$1/4$ cup walnut pieces, toasted on a baking sheet in a single layer for 7 to 8 minutes in a 375°F. oven

$1/4$ cup heavy cream

1 recipe Fresh Pasta Dough (page 140) or 1 pound dried fettuccine

Cornmeal, for dusting

All-purpose flour, for rolling

In a small bowl, cover the dried mushrooms with $1/2$ cup of boiling water and set aside for 30 minutes to hydrate. Drain, reserving the soaking liquid.

In the meantime, in a large saucepan, heat a 2-count of olive oil over medium heat. Toss in the fresh mushrooms, garlic, celery, and sage and season with salt and a few grinds of fresh black pepper. Sauté for 12 to 15 minutes, until the mushrooms have browned slightly. Add the drained, dried porcinis and cook 2 more minutes. Now dump the mushroom mixture into the food processor. Add $1/4$ cup of the grated cheese and the toasted walnuts and purée, then return the mixture to the pan. Add the dried-mushroom soaking liquid and the cream and give it a stir. Take the sauce off the heat; set it aside while you roll and cut the pasta.

Bring a big pot of lightly salted water to a boil for the pasta.

If using fresh pasta, get yourself a baking sheet and dust it with cornmeal. When it has rested, cut the ball of dough into big chunks. Cover and reserve the dough you are not immediately using to keep it from drying out. Dust the counter and the dough with a little flour. Roll the chunk of dough through a pasta machine at the widest setting; you'll have a strip. Fold that strip in half, turn it 90 degrees, and roll it through again. Now you have nice, straight edges. Roll the dough another two or three times in the same direction, pulling and stretching it with the palm of your hand as you gently pull it out from the rollers. Crank the setting down, and roll the dough through again, two or three times. Continue tightening and rolling, one setting at a time, until the machine is at the thinnest setting. Now put the pasta-cutting attachment on the machine and cut the dough into wide noodles. Put the noodles on the cornmeal-dusted baking sheet and roll and cut the rest of the dough chunks.

Drop the pasta into the boiling water and cook until al dente, 2 or 3 minutes for fresh (8 or 9 minutes for dried). Drain and then put the pasta into a big bowl. Warm the sauce over medium heat. Season with salt and pepper. Pour the sauce over the drained pasta and toss to coat. Shower with the rest of the Pecorino and serve hot.

Penne Puttanesca

45 minutes + 45 minutes if using fresh pasta | Serves 4

Pasta Puttanesca, or "whore's" pasta, is a classic recipe from the back streets of Naples. It owes its colorful name to the fact that it is easy, fast, and delicious like a beautiful Napolitana woman.

Put a large saucepan over medium heat and add the olive oil. Add the garlic and anchovies and cook, using a wooden spoon to break up the anchovies until they seem to dissolve in the oil. Add the olives, red pepper flakes, and capers, and let that cook for 2 minutes, stirring often.

Toss in the tomatoes with their juices and bring to a low simmer. Stir in the basil and season with salt and pepper. Simmer for 10 minutes. Remove from the heat and stir in the grated cheese.

Bring a big pot of lightly salted water to a boil for the pasta.

If using fresh pasta, get yourself a baking sheet and dust it with cornmeal. Cut the ball of dough into big chunks. Cover and reserve the pieces you're not using right away to keep them from drying out. Dust the counter and the dough with a little flour. Roll the chunk of dough through a pasta machine at the widest setting; you'll have a strip. Fold that strip in half, turn it 90 degrees, and roll it through again. Now you have nice, straight edges. Roll the dough another two or three times in the same direction, pulling and stretching it with the palm of your hand as you gently guide it from the rollers. Crank the setting down, and roll the dough through again, two or three times. Continue tightening and rolling, one setting at a time, until the machine is at the thinnest setting. Cut the sheet of dough into 2-inch squares. Wrap each square around the handle of a wooden spoon and use a dab of water to seal into a tubular shape. (Wrap the dough at a slight angle so that the ends of the penne are pointed, like quills.) Roll the penne off the spoon handle onto the cornmeal-dusted baking sheet. Continue to roll and shape all of the dough.

Drop the fresh pasta into the boiling water and cook until al dente, 2 or 3 minutes for fresh (7 or 8 minutes for dried). Drain and dump it into a big pasta bowl. At the same time, bring the sauce back to a simmer. Pour it over the drained pasta and toss to coat. Serve immediately.

$1/3$ cup extra-virgin olive oil

3 garlic cloves, minced

6 anchovies, rinsed

1 cup black olives, pitted and roughly chopped

1 teaspoon dried red pepper flakes

3 tablespoons capers, drained

2 (28-ounce) cans whole, peeled tomatoes, preferably San Marzano style, crushed by hand

$1/4$ cup fresh basil leaves, hand torn

Kosher salt and freshly ground black pepper

$1/3$ cup freshly grated Pecorino or Parmigiano-Reggiano cheese

1 recipe Fresh Pasta Dough (page 140) or 1 pound dried penne

Cornmeal, for dusting

All-purpose flour, for rolling

Linguine with White Clam Sauce

45 minutes + 45 minutes if using fresh pasta | Serves 4 to 6

This is probably one of the quickest pasta recipes in my repertoire. It also happens to be delicious. Make sure you give the clams a good scrub before you start.

1 recipe Fresh Pasta Dough (page 140) or 1 pound dried linguine

Cornmeal, for dusting

All-purpose flour, for rolling

$\frac{1}{4}$ cup extra-virgin olive oil, plus extra for drizzling

4 garlic cloves, slivered

$\frac{1}{4}$ teaspoon dried red pepper flakes

2 pounds small littleneck or Manila clams, scrubbed and rinsed well

$\frac{3}{4}$ cup dry white wine, such as Pinot Grigio

Juice of 1 lemon

3 tablespoons unsalted butter

Kosher salt and freshly ground black pepper

2 handfuls of fresh flat-leaf parsley, finely chopped

2 tablespoons lightly toasted bread crumbs (optional)

Bring a large pot of lightly salted water to a boil.

If using fresh pasta, get yourself a baking sheet and dust it with cornmeal. Cut the ball of dough into big chunks. Cover and reserve the pieces you're not using right away to keep it from drying out. Dust the counter and the dough with a little flour. Roll the chunk of dough through a pasta machine at the widest setting; you'll have a strip. Fold that strip in half, turn it 90 degrees, and roll it through again. Now you have nice, straight edges. Roll the dough another two or three times in the same direction, pulling and stretching it with the palm of your hand as it emerges from the rollers. Crank the setting down, and roll the dough through again, two or three times. Continue tightening and rolling, one setting at a time, until the machine is at the thinnest setting. Now put the pasta-cutting attachment on the machine and cut the dough into thin noodles. Put the noodles on the cornmeal-dusted baking sheet and continue to roll and cut all of the pasta.

Heat the olive oil over medium heat in a deep sauté pan with a lid. Add the garlic and sauté for 2 minutes to soften. Add the red pepper flakes and cook for about 3 minutes. Add the clams, wine, and lemon juice. Cover and cook, shaking the pan periodically, until the clams have opened, about 7 minutes. Discard any clams that don't open.

A few minutes before the clams are cooked, drop your pasta into the boiling water and cook until al dente, 2 to 3 minutes for fresh (7 to 8 minutes for dried). Drain the pasta well and put it in a big pasta bowl.

Now crank the heat up to medium-high under the sauce and get it good and hot. Pour over the hot pasta. Toss in the butter and season with salt and pepper. Toss the pasta with the clams until it's all nicely coated. Shower with chopped parsley and toasted bread crumbs, if you like, and drizzle it with olive oil before serving.

Ligurian Lasagna

45 minutes + 45 minutes to make the dough and let it rest | Serves 4

This style of lasagna comes from Genoa, on the Ligurian coast. It is traditionally served at room temperature because the climate in that part of Italy is quite warm throughout the year. When the warm, cooked pasta sheets are stacked together with the pesto, green beans, and potatoes, the pasta gently warms the pesto and heightens its natural flavor while keeping the color a beautiful green. The final step is to cook the pasta so it is still warm when you assemble the lasagna.

First get the potatoes going. Don't peel them—they'll lose flavor and absorb a lot of water if you do. Put the potatoes in a saucepan, cover with cold water and add enough salt to make the water taste slightly salty. Bring to a boil, reduce the heat, and simmer until the potatoes are cooked through, 15 to 20 minutes. Drain, and set aside on a plate until cool enough to handle, then peel and break into pieces; set aside.

Meanwhile, cook the beans, too. Bring a large pot of salted water to a boil. Fill a large bowl with ice water and add salt until it tastes slightly salty. When the water comes to a boil, add the beans and cook until just tender, about 3 minutes. Remove with a slotted spoon (you'll use the same pot to cook the pasta), then refresh in the water bath to keep the bright green color, and drain well; set aside.

Now make the pesto. Put the garlic, pine nuts, and oil in a food processor and purée. Add the basil and process again to purée. Add the ricotta, the yogurt, and the Pecorino cheese and process just until combined. Set aside.

For the pasta, cut the ball of dough in half. Cover and reserve the piece you are not immediately using to prevent it from drying out. Dust the counter and dough with a little flour. Roll the chunk of dough through a pasta machine at the widest setting; you'll have a strip. Fold that strip in half, turn 90 degrees, and roll it through again. Now you have nice, straight edges. Roll the dough another two or three times in the same direction. Pull and stretch the sheet of dough with the palm of your hand as it emerges from the rollers. Reduce the setting and crank the dough through again, two or three times. Continue tightening and rolling, one setting at a time, until the machine is at the thinnest setting so that you have a very long, thin sheet of dough. Cut that in half width-

{ recipe continues }

1 pound small Yukon Gold potatoes
Kosher salt
1 pound haricots verts or young
   green beans, trimmed

PESTO
2 garlic cloves
1/4 cup pine nuts
1/2 cup extra-virgin olive oil
Leaves from 2 large bunches of
   fresh basil, stemmed
2 cups of the best ricotta cheese
   you can find
1 tablespoon plain yogurt
1/2 cup freshly grated Pecorino
   cheese

1 pound Fresh Pasta Dough
   (page 140)
Extra-virgin olive oil
1/2 cup freshly grated Pecorino
   cheese

wise and put both pieces on a cornmeal-dusted baking sheet. Do the same with the second piece of dough so that you have four equal strips of pasta.

Bring your water back to a boil. Drop two of the strips into the boiling water and cook for 2 minutes. Remove with a slotted spoon, drain, and put them on large plate; drizzle with olive oil. Cook the remaining two strips of pasta the same way and put them on the same plate, drizzling each with olive oil so that the pasta gets really drenched with the taste of the oil. Cover with a towel to keep warm.

To assemble, take a platter large enough to hold one sheet of pasta in a single layer and spread with about one-fifth of the pesto directly on the platter. Sprinkle with a quarter of the green beans and potatoes and a quarter of the Pecorino cheese. Repeat that three more times to use all of the pasta sheets, pesto, vegetables, and cheese, ending with a layer of pesto. Cut into portions with a knife or spatula and serve at room temperature.

Spaghetti alla Carbonara

45 minutes + 45 minutes if using fresh pasta | Serves 4

The trick here is to get the sauce ingredients ready while the pasta is cooking so that you can take the hot pasta directly from the colander to the bowl with the pancetta and then throw the raw eggs on top; it's only the heat of the pasta that cooks the eggs.

Bring a big pot of lightly salted water to a boil for the pasta.

If using fresh pasta, get yourself a baking sheet and dust it with cornmeal. When the pasta dough has rested, cut the ball into big chunks. Cover and reserve the pieces you're not going to use right away to keep them from drying out. Dust the counter and the dough with a little flour. Roll the chunk of dough through a pasta machine at the widest setting; you'll have a strip. Fold that strip in half, turn it 90 degrees, and roll it through again. Now you have nice, straight edges. Roll the dough another two or three times in the same direction, pulling and stretching it with the palm of your hand as you're pulling it out from the rollers. Crank the setting down, and roll the dough through again, two or three times. Continue tightening and rolling, one setting at a time, until the machine is at the thinnest setting. Now put the pasta-cutting attachment on the machine and cut the dough into thin noodles. Put the noodles on the cornmeal-dusted baking sheet and keep going to roll and cut all of the pasta.

Heat a 2-count of olive oil in a deep skillet over medium heat. Add the pancetta and sauté for about 3 minutes, until crispy; you're looking to extract the pork fat. Toss the garlic into the fat and sauté for just under a minute to soften. Scrape everything into a big pasta bowl. Beat the eggs and Parmigiano in a mixing bowl, stirring well to break up any lumps.

Now drop the pasta into the boiling water and cook until al dente—tender yet firm—2 to 3 minutes for fresh (8 to 9 minutes for dried). Drain the pasta well, reserving $1/2$ cup of the starchy cooking water.

Add the hot, drained spaghetti to the bowl with the pancetta and toss for 2 minutes to coat the strands in the pork fat. Pour the egg–cheese mixture onto the hot pasta, tossing quickly with a fork until the eggs thicken (this is done off the heat to prevent scrambling). Thin out the sauce with a bit of the reserved pasta water, if you need to. Season with lots of freshly ground black pepper and taste for salt. Garnish with the chopped parsley. Pass more cheese around the table.

1 recipe Fresh Pasta Dough (page 140) or 1 pound dried spaghetti

Cornmeal, for dusting

All-purpose flour, for rolling

Extra-virgin olive oil

4 ounces pancetta or slab bacon, cubed or sliced into small strips

4 garlic cloves, finely chopped

4 large eggs

1 cup freshly grated Parmigiano-Reggiano cheese, plus more for serving

Kosher salt and freshly ground black pepper

1 handful of fresh flat-leaf parsley, chopped

Ravioli with Sweet Crab and Green Herb Sauce

1 ¼ hours + 45 minutes to make the dough and let it rest | Makes 24 ravioli

When crab is impeccably fresh, I prefer to add only a few ingredients to heighten the crab's own natural flavor. Lemon juice, olive oil, and salt usually do the trick. This recipe is written using Dungeness crabmeat, but whatever kind of fresh crab you can find will be perfect. Just spend a couple of minutes picking through it to get rid of any bits of shell.

1 recipe Fresh Pasta Dough (page 140)

FILLING

1 pound Dungeness crabmeat, picked through for shells

2 tablespoons extra-virgin olive oil

Juice of ½ lemon

1 large egg white

Kosher salt and freshly ground black pepper

SAUCE

4 cups (packed) mixed fresh herbs, such as parsley, basil, tarragon, and mint

4 green onions, green parts only, chopped

Zest of 1 lemon, finely grated

Kosher salt and freshly ground black pepper

Extra-virgin olive oil

3 anchovy fillets

3 garlic cloves, minced

¼ cup heavy cream

{ ingredients continue }

While the pasta dough is resting, make the ravioli filling. In a bowl, stir together the crab, oil, lemon juice, egg white, and salt and pepper. Cover that and stick it in the refrigerator until you're ready to use it.

Now make the sauce. In the bowl of a food processor, put your herbs, green onions, lemon zest, and salt and pepper. Pulse to chop it all up a bit. Add about ½ cup of olive oil and purée it down until it's smooth and bright green. Coat a wide sauté pan with a 2-count of olive oil and put it over medium heat. When the oil gets hazy, add the anchovies and mash them up with a wooden spoon so they melt into the oil. Toss in the garlic and stir it around until it just begins to turn golden, not brown. Carefully pour in the herb purée, stirring to incorporate. Mix in the heavy cream and season with salt and pepper. Now you're ready to make the raviolis. Set the sauce aside and go back to the dough.

Cut the ball of dough into big chunks. Cover and reserve the pieces you are not immediately using to prevent them from drying out. Dust the counter and dough with a little flour. Roll the chunk of dough through a pasta machine at the widest setting; you'll have a strip. Fold that strip in half, turn it 90 degrees, and roll it through again. Now you have a nice edge. Roll the dough another two or three times in the same direction, pulling and stretching it with the palm of your hand as it emerges from the rollers. Crank the setting down, and roll the dough through again, two or three times. Continue tightening and rolling, one setting at a time, until the machine is at the thinnest setting. Roll out the remaining chunks of dough.

Bring a big pot of lightly salted water to a boil for the ravioli. Dust a baking sheet with cornmeal.

Beat the egg with 1 tablespoon of water to make an egg wash. Dust the counter and dough with flour, lay out a long sheet of pasta, and brush the top surface with the egg wash, which acts as a glue. Drop the filling by tablespoonfuls on the top half of the pasta sheet, about 2 inches apart. Fold the bottom half over the filling like a blanket. With an espresso cup or your fingers, gently press out air pockets around each mound of filling. Use a sharp knife to cut each pillow into squares and crimp the four edges with the tines of a fork to make a tight seal. Dust the ravioli with cornmeal to prevent the pasta from sticking and lay them out on the cornmeal-dusted baking sheet to dry slightly while assembling the rest.

Drop the ravioli in the boiling salted water and cook for 4 minutes; they'll float to the top when ready, so be careful not to overcrowd the pot. Lift the ravioli from the water with a large strainer or slotted spoon. Warm the sauce over low heat, add the ravioli, and toss gently to coat with the sauce. Serve immediately.

All-purpose flour, for rolling
Kosher salt
Cornmeal, for dusting
1 egg, for egg wash

TASTING

When the weather finally starts to warm up after a long, cold winter, the downtown farmers' market in New York City starts bustling with a **NEW RHYTHM.** The market goes from maybe ten stalls to about one hundred, in a week. Then, as if there were a friendly competition, local growers display an **EYE-POPPING ARRAY OF PRODUCE**, each claiming to have the best, the freshest, the most organic. I buy a tomato from one of the stalls and eat it standing there, as if it were an apple, and every year it's like tasting a tomato for the very first time. **SUMMERTIME IS MY FAVORITE TIME OF THE YEAR TO COOK** because the produce is so great. Summer tastes like cold, sliced tomatoes with salt, and like fresh corn; it tastes the way a garden smells, like lemon curd and blueberries. The recipes in this chapter are my summer collection hit list. The recipes are easy to put together and they truly **TASTE LIKE THE SUN.**

Spanish Gazpacho

45 minutes + at least 2 hours to chill | Serves 6

Here's the story. There was a couple who were living in Spain while the husband was in the U.S. Air Force. Stationed there for three or four years, they had both fallen in love with the classic, sunny flavors of Spain. Fast forward, ten years later. He's taken a desk job in D.C. They live in the suburbs of Bethesda and there's not a Spanish restaurant for miles. Here's the cure: authentic Spanish gazpacho. I whipped up this recipe with them one afternoon. I think you're going to love it, too.

Remove the crusts from the bread. Pour 1 cup of water over the bread in a bowl and let it soak for 5 minutes. (The bread will give the soup a little body without adding fat.) Squeeze out the water and put the bread in a blender or food processor. Add the tomatoes, cucumbers, bell pepper, onion, and garlic. Purée the whole thing until it's almost smooth but still has a little texture. Pour the purée into a large bowl and stir in the tomato juice, sugar, paprika, vinegar, oil, parsley, lemon juice, and salt and pepper to taste.

Now you want to refrigerate the soup for at least 2 hours so it gets very well chilled. The flavors will develop while the soup sits. Before you serve it, taste the gazpacho and season it again with salt and pepper (chilled food always needs a little more seasoning). Serve in chilled bowls or a tureen and pass small bowls of chopped garnishes.

3 slices day-old French bread

2 pounds ripe tomatoes, seeded and coarsely chopped

2 small Kirby cucumbers, coarsely chopped

1 red or yellow bell pepper, cored, seeded, and coarsely chopped

1 medium onion, coarsely chopped

2 garlic cloves, chopped

2 cups tomato juice or water

1 tablespoon sugar

1 tablespoon Spanish paprika

$^{1}/_{4}$ cup sherry vinegar

$^{1}/_{2}$ cup extra-virgin olive oil

1 handful of fresh flat-leaf parsley, coarsely chopped

Juice of $^{1}/_{2}$ lemon

Kosher salt and freshly ground black pepper

GARNISHES

2 ripe tomatoes, chopped

2 Kirby cucumbers, chopped

1 red bell pepper, cored, seeded, and chopped

1 small onion, chopped

2 hard-cooked eggs, chopped

Lemon wedges

Roasted Corn with Parmesan and Cayenne

45 minutes | Serves 8

This is street food in Mexico City but it's easy to pull off at home. The corn can also be charred over a gas flame or under the broiler.

8 ears fresh corn, in the husk

1 cup mayonnaise, homemade
(see page 15) or store-bought

1 cup freshly grated Parmigiano-
Reggiano cheese

Cayenne pepper

Lime wedges, for serving

Preheat the oven to 350°F. Place the corn, still in its husks, directly on the oven rack and roast for about 20 minutes, until the corn is soft when you press on it. Take the corn out of the oven and let it cool a little until you can handle it, or until you're ready to serve.

When you're ready to eat, place a large grill pan on two burners over medium-high heat or preheat an outdoor gas or charcoal grill and get it very hot. Take a few paper towels and fold them several times to make a thick square. Blot a small amount of oil on the paper towels. Then carefully and quickly wipe the hot grates of the grill to make a nonstick grilling surface. When the grill pan or grill is hot, peel down the husks from the roasted corn and pull out the corn silk. Then tie the husks in a knot like a handle. Char the corn on the grill pan or grill, turning, until the kernels are slightly blackened all around and start popping, about 6 minutes. Brush the corn with mayonnaise, and sprinkle with the Parmigiano cheese and a little cayenne pepper. Serve with lime wedges.

Avocado Salad with Lemon, Bacon, and Watercress

30 minutes | Serves 4 to 6

I just happened to put these ingredients together one night last summer, and I'm telling you it felt like I tasted peanut butter and jelly for the first time. Simple flavors and ingredients that just taste great together and unbelievably, the most difficult step is cooking the bacon.

$^1/_2$ pound sliced bacon

3 avocados, split, pitted, and peeled

Juice of 1 lemon

$^1/_4$ cup extra-virgin olive oil

Kosher salt and freshly ground
black pepper

$^1/_2$ bunch of watercress, stems
trimmed

Preheat the oven to 375°F. Lay the bacon on a baking sheet lined with parchment and bake for 15 minutes, until crispy. Transfer the bacon to a plate lined with paper towels and let it drain for a couple of minutes.

Break or cut the avocados into chunks and arrange on a platter. Drizzle with the lemon juice and olive oil. Sprinkle with salt and pepper. Scatter the watercress over the avocado and top with the bacon.

Ham Quiche with Herb and Asparagus Salad

1 hour + baking time | Serves 10 to 12

Baked in a springform pan, this quiche has the height of a cheesecake. It's perfect for outdoor entertaining in the summer and a real show stopper for when the in-laws come over.

PASTRY

2 cups all-purpose flour, plus
　　more for dusting

1 teaspoon kosher salt

¼ teaspoon sugar

¾ cup (1 ½ sticks) cold unsalted
　　butter, cut into small chunks

1 large egg yolk

3 tablespoons ice water, plus
　　more if needed

FILLING

3 tablespoons extra-virgin olive oil

2 large Vidalia or other sweet onions,
　　sliced

¾ pound smoked ham, cubed

Kosher salt and freshly ground
　　black pepper

8 large eggs

1 quart heavy cream

To make the pastry, combine the flour, salt, and sugar in a large mixing bowl. Add the butter and mix with a pastry blender or rub between your hands until the mixture resembles coarse crumbs. In a small bowl, combine the egg yolk and ice water and mix together with a fork. Add the liquids to the flour and work them in to bind until the dough holds together without being too wet or sticky. Squeeze a small amount in your palm: If it is crumbly, add more ice water 1 tablespoon at a time. Form the dough into a disk and wrap in plastic wrap. Refrigerate for at least 30 minutes.

While the dough chills, work on the filling. Put a skillet over medium-low heat. Drizzle with a 3-count of oil. Add the onions and cook slowly, stirring, until they caramelize and release their natural sugars, 15 to 20 minutes. Add a couple of tablespoons of water to help the onions break down, if needed. Toss in the ham and cook, stirring, for about 10 minutes to get some color on it, too. Remove the pan from the heat and season with salt and pepper. In a large bowl, beat the eggs until frothy. Pour in the cream and season well with salt and pepper.

By now, the dough will be ready to roll and bake. Preheat the oven to 375°F. Sprinkle the counter and a rolling pin lightly with flour. Roll the dough out to a 14-inch circle about ¼ inch thick. Carefully roll the dough up onto the pin (this may take a little practice) and lay it inside a 9-inch springform pan. Press the dough firmly into the bottom and sides of the pan so it fits tightly. Trim the excess dough around the rim and put the pan on a sturdy cookie sheet so it will be easier to move in and out of the oven. (This quiche is pretty heavy.) Arrange the caramelized onions and ham over the bottom of the pie shell and carefully pour in the cream-and-egg mixture. The filling should come all the way up to about 1 inch from the top of the pan. Cover with foil and bake for 1 hour and 30 minutes, or until the quiche is set and puffy and jiggles slightly. Remove the foil during the last 15 minutes of baking. Remove the quiche to a wire rack and let cool for 30 minutes.

When the quiche is just about cool, make the asparagus salad. In a large pot of boiling salted water, blanch the asparagus for 4 minutes, or until they are just crisp-tender. Drain, transfer to a bowl of ice water to stop the cooking, and drain again. Cut the asparagus into 1/2-inch pieces and put them in a large bowl. Add the cheese and herbs and toss everything together. Drizzle with olive oil, give it a squeeze of lemon juice, and season with salt and pepper.

Loosen the cooled quiche from the sides of the pan by running a thin metal spatula around the inside rim. Carefully remove the ring, and transfer the quiche (with the bottom base) to a serving plate. Cut into wedges, drizzle with a little olive oil, and season with a few turns of pepper. Arrange some of the asparagus salad on top of each wedge and serve.

SALAD

2 pounds asparagus, stems trimmed

1/2 cup Parmigiano-Reggiano cheese, shaved with a vegetable peeler

2 handfuls of flat-leaf parsley leaves, torn if very large

1 handful of fresh mint leaves, torn if very large

1 handful of fresh dill sprigs

Extra-virgin olive oil

Juice of 1/2 lemon

Kosher salt and freshly ground black pepper

Salade Niçoise with Seared Tuna

1 hour | Serves 4

This plate tastes like summer to me. When the weather starts to warm up, I look forward to squeezing it onto a menu somewhere. Delicious rich tuna, salty olives, and fresh herbs take me straight to the coast.

First make the vinaigrette by putting all of the ingredients into a jar. Screw on the cap and shake it all up vigorously to emulsify the oil and vinegar. Set the vinaigrette aside while you make the salad; this gives the flavors a little time to marry.

Fill a large bowl with ice water and add salt to it until it tastes lightly salty. You can cut down on prep time and cleanup by cooking the potatoes, eggs, and green beans in the same pot. Start with the potatoes because they take the longest to cook. Find a large pot with a steamer basket that fits inside. (It should suspend over the top of the pan, 5 to 6 inches from the bottom.) Setting the steamer basket aside for now, put the potatoes in the pot, add water to cover, and throw in a nice pinch of salt. Bring to a boil over medium heat and simmer for 12 to 15 minutes, until the potatoes are just beginning to soften.

Now gently slide the eggs into the simmering water and set a timer for 10 minutes. Place the steamer basket on top (it shouldn't touch the simmering water). Put the green beans in the steamer and cover the whole thing with a lid. Steam the beans for 5 minutes or until crisp-tender while the potatoes continue to cook until fork tender. When you remove the steamer basket with the beans, check the potatoes. If they're cooked, take them out; if not, let them keep cooking until tender. Take the eggs out when the timer rings; they cook in exactly 10 minutes. Place the potatoes, eggs, and green beans in the ice water to cool, then rinse under cold water in a colander. Peel the shells off the eggs and cut them in half lengthwise. Set the eggs and vegetables aside.

Put a large skillet over medium-high heat and add 1 tablespoon olive oil. Rub the tuna on all sides with a drizzle of oil and a bit of the vinaigrette, and season with a fair amount of salt and pepper. When the oil is smoking hot, lay the tuna in the pan and sear for approximately 2 minutes on each side. As the tuna cooks, you'll see the red meat begin to whiten; you want the center of the tuna to remain rare and red. Transfer the tuna to a cutting board and slice it about $1/2$ inch thick.

{ **recipe continues** }

VINAIGRETTE

1 garlic clove, minced

1 teaspoon Dijon mustard

1 $1/2$ tablespoons red wine vinegar

Juice of $1/2$ lemon

1 tablespoon chopped fresh flat-leaf parsley

$1/2$ tablespoon minced fresh tarragon

Kosher salt and freshly ground black pepper

$1/4$ cup extra-virgin olive oil

SALAD

Kosher salt and freshly ground black pepper

$1/2$ pound small red new potatoes, scrubbed and halved

4 large eggs

$1/4$ pound haricots verts or green beans, stems trimmed

Extra-virgin olive oil

1 pound sushi-quality tuna

5 ounces mixed baby greens

$1/2$ pint teardrop or cherry tomatoes, halved

$1/2$ cup Niçoise olives

8 anchovy fillets

8 caper berries with stems or 1 tablespoon capers, drained

$1/4$ bunch of fresh chives, snipped in half

Then get a large mixing bowl and put the potatoes, green beans, mixed greens, tomatoes, olives, anchovies, caper berries, and chives into it. Give the vinaigrette another good shake to emulsify and then drizzle the salad with enough vinaigrette to fully moisten everything. Toss gently to coat. Season with salt and pepper. (Take care not to mush up the ingredients; the important thing about salade niçoise is that it be arranged beautifully on a platter, with all the ingredients intact.)

Arrange the tossed salad down the center of a serving platter and lay the seared tuna attractively across the top. Set the eggs around the rim. Drizzle with the remaining vinaigrette and serve.

Summer Tomatoes, Slashed and Stuffed
About 30 minutes | Serves 4 to 6

The smell of a tomato plant at the height of summer is hypnotic, and nothing screams summer like fresh tomatoes. Once they're picked, however, tomatoes taste about as good as they're going to. If you can't find tomatoes in your backyard, buying them on the vine is the next best thing. In this particular recipe, I roasted the tomatoes on the vine. And with butter and basil, they taste like sweet tomato sauce.

**6 ripe tomatoes on the vine
(2 to 3 pounds)**
6 tablespoons unsalted butter
6 fresh basil leaves
Extra-virgin olive oil
**Kosher salt and freshly ground
black pepper**

Preheat the oven to 425°F. Put the tomatoes in a baking dish and make a shallow slash in each tomato right by the stem. Poke a finger into the tomato to make a hole and stuff with 1 tablespoon of butter and a basil leaf. Coat the tomatoes with olive oil, sprinkle with salt and pepper, and roast until the skins begin to shrivel and the tomatoes are warmed through, 20 to 30 minutes, depending on size.

Summer Bean Salad with Creamy Lemon Dressing

30 minutes | Serves 6

I came up with this recipe last summer. I was strolling through the Union Square Greenmarket in New York City and I came across these really cool summer beans—yellow wax beans and beautiful haricots verts. I put together a simple vinaigrette with the things I had in my pantry: lemon juice, mustard, and crème fraîche. Green beans taste like a cool drink of water to me —grassy and cool. I took the bowl and sat on my fire escape in the hot July sun and had a picnic.

Bring a large pot of salted water to a boil. Add all of the beans and cook until crisp-tender, 3 to 5 minutes (they'll all be done at roughly the same time). Drain, transfer to a bowl of salted ice water to stop the cooking, and drain well. Transfer to a mixing bowl and toss in the shallots, walnuts, and parsley.

In a jar, combine the mustard, water, sugar, lemon juice, oil, crème fraîche, salt, and pepper. Put the cap on and shake vigorously to emulsify. Just before you serve the salad, pour the dressing over the beans and toss well to coat with the dressing.

NOTE | Toast walnuts on a baking sheet in a 375°F. oven for 7 to 8 minutes, until fragrant.

1 pound mixed summer beans, such as sugar snap peas, haricots verts or green beans, yellow wax beans, or runner beans, stems trimmed

1 ^{1}/$_2$ shallots, finely chopped

^{1}/$_2$ cup walnut halves and pieces, toasted (see Note)

1 handful of fresh flat-leaf parsley, chopped

1 tablespoon grainy mustard

1 tablespoon hot water

^{1}/$_2$ teaspoon sugar

Juice of 1 lemon

^{1}/$_3$ cup extra-virgin olive oil

^{1}/$_4$ cup crème fraîche or sour cream

Kosher salt and freshly ground black pepper

Carpaccio of Raw Zucchini

30 minutes | Serves 4 to 6

I put this dish together when we were on location for *Tyler's Ultimate*. We were breaking for lunch and I raided the refrigerator of the lady we were working with. I just pulled a couple of ingredients out and started to try to figure out how to turn it all into a salad. It was a bit "loaves and fishes," meaning that I didn't have a lot to work with. I sliced zucchini very thin, spread it out around the plate, and seasoned it with a little salt and olive oil, and the zucchini melted and got juicy. Then I tried to figure out how to make it better: A little leek, a little fresh herb, a little ricotta cheese, and a squeeze of lemon juice on top. It tasted so amazing that I thought, this is one for the book.

The secret to this dish is that the zucchini be sliced as thin as possible (a plastic Japanese mandoline does a nice job) so that the squash takes up the flavor of the lemon and herbs.

2 zucchini (about 1 $^1/_2$ pounds total), sliced into paper-thin rounds

Kosher salt and freshly ground black pepper

Extra-virgin olive oil

Juice of $^1/_2$ lemon

$^1/_4$ cup chopped fresh herbs, such as chervil, dill, chives, and chive blossoms

1 young leek, white part only, sliced paper-thin

1 cup ricotta cheese

Fresh mint leaves, for garnish

Shingle the zucchini slices in a single overlapping layer on a platter. Dust with salt and pepper, then drizzle with a 3-count of olive oil and the lemon juice. Sprinkle with the herbs. Now scatter the leek over. Put that in the fridge for about 10 minutes to give the flavors a chance to get into the zucchini. Then garnish with the ricotta cheese and mint leaves.

Panzanella

1 hour | Serves 4 to 6

When I was nineteen years old and the chef (well, if you want to call it that—it was me and a dishwasher six nights a week) at this little Italian place in my hometown, I came across a recipe for panzanella in an old, out-of-print Italian cookbook and fell in love with the sheer simplicity of it. Panzanella was one of my first experiences of how truly simple great Italian food can be.

Preheat the oven to 400°F. Toss the bread chunks with ¼ cup oil until the bread is wet with the oil. Spread the bread on a baking sheet and bake until the bread begins to brown, about 10 minutes.

While the bread is going, make the dressing. Use a large knife to chop and mash the garlic, anchovies, and salt to a paste on a cutting board. Scrape it into a large mixing bowl, add the lemon juice, vinegar, oil, salt, and pepper, and stir together. Add all of the rest of the ingredients and gently stir. Taste for seasoning. Finally, add the toasted bread and toss it all together. Taste it and season one last time with salt, pepper, and lemon juice.

1 French boule, or loaf of
   round Tuscan bread, torn into
   bite-size pieces
Extra-virgin olive oil
2 garlic cloves
3 anchovy fillets
Kosher salt and freshly ground
   black pepper
Juice of ½ lemon, or as needed
2 tablespoons red wine vinegar
1 tablespoon capers, drained
2 roasted red bell peppers (see page
   181), shredded by hand
½ pint red cherry tomatoes, halved
½ pint yellow cherry tomatoes,
   halved
½ red onion, finely chopped
1 seedless cucumber, peeled and
   cut into ½-inch cubes
½ bunch of basil, torn into
   largish pieces
¼ cup celery leaves, torn into
   largish pieces

I LIKE TO GIVE FISH A QUICK MARINADE
BEFORE I GRILL IT. I JUST CHOP THE INGREDIENTS
TOGETHER AND SQUEEZE THEM OVER THE FISH.
AN HOUR IN THAT MARINADE AND A FEW MINUTES
ON THE GRILL, AND NEXT THING YOU KNOW
YOU'RE TASTING THE MEDITERRANEAN.

Grilled Branzino with Fennel and Tangerines

45 minutes + 1 hour to marinate | Serves 4

Branzino is a fish that I've eaten abroad but I've recently seen it in fish markets all over the place. It's a Mediterranean sea bass. When it's grilled, it has a soft, delicate oceany flavor, and the skin gets very crisp. It's also loaded with omega-3 oil. I think it's my new favorite fish. I paired its flavors with crisp, raw fennel and citrus. When you taste this recipe, it's undeniably summer.

4 whole branzino (about 1 pound each), filleted to yield 8 small fillets, or 4 larger fillets (6 to 8 ounces) of whatever fish you'd like (salmon, striped bass, snapper)

1 tablespoon fennel seeds

2 teaspoons black peppercorns

3 tangerines

Extra-virgin olive oil

Kosher salt and freshly ground black pepper

2 fennel bulbs, trimmed and thinly sliced, fronds reserved for garnish

Juice of $^{1}/_{2}$ lemon

$^{1}/_{4}$ cup chopped fresh flat-leaf parsley

Put the fillets in a baking dish large enough to hold them in a single layer. Put the fennel seeds and peppercorns on a cutting board and whack with the bottom of a heavy pan to crack them; sprinkle the cracked spices over the fish. Remove a strip of zest from one of the tangerines with a zester or microplane and add it to the dish. Pour $^{1}/_{2}$ cup of olive oil over the fish and let it all marinate for 1 hour.

Cut off the top and bottom ends of the tangerines so that they stand upright. Then use a knife to cut off the peels in long strips, including as much of the bitter white pith as possible. Cut between the membranes to free the sections; remove the seeds and set the sections aside in a medium bowl. Discard the membranes.

Place a large grill pan on two burners over medium-high heat or preheat an outdoor gas or charcoal grill and get it very hot. Take a few paper towels and fold them several times to make a square. Blot a small amount of oil on the paper towels and then carefully and quickly wipe the hot grates of the grill (or the ridges of the grill pan) to create a nonstick surface. Sprinkle the fish with salt. Put it on the grill and cook, turning once, until just cooked through but a little translucent in the center, 4 to 5 minutes total for thinner fillets, 8 to 12 minutes for thicker fillets.

To finish, take your bowl with the tangerine sections, add the fennel, 3 tablespoons of olive oil, the lemon juice, parsley, fennel fronds, and salt and pepper to taste, and toss. Arrange the salad on a platter, put the fish on top, and serve.

Grilled Shrimp Salad with Black-Eyed Peas and Citrus-Chile Vinaigrette

1 hour | Serves 6 to 8

This is a dish that really stands up to my southern roots. After culinary school, I worked the restaurant circuit in Charleston. Fresh coastal shrimp, creamy black-eyed peas, citrus, and chiles are classic Low Country flavors.

First get the peas going. Put a 2-gallon stockpot over medium heat. Drizzle with a 2-count of olive oil, add the garlic and jalapeño, and sauté until the vegetables are soft, about 3 minutes. Add the black-eyed peas, ham hocks, bay leaves, and 2 quarts of water. Bring to a boil, reduce the heat, and simmer for 45 minutes, or until the peas are tender, stirring when you think about it. Wait until halfway through cooking to begin seasoning with salt and pepper. You want the peas to break down a little bit so the seasoning can penetrate the flesh inside. Drain the black-eyed peas, put them in a bowl, and toss with half of the vinaigrette. Shred the ham hocks; set the meat aside separately. Discard the bones and bay leaves.

Now put the shrimp in a glass bowl and add the chili powder, olive oil, lime juice, the ½ handful of cilantro, and a good pinch each of salt and pepper. Mix that all up well and let it marinate for 15 minutes while you heat up the grill. Place a large grill pan on two burners over medium-high heat or preheat an outdoor gas or charcoal grill. Fold a few paper towels into a thick square. Blot some oil on the paper towels and then carefully and quickly wipe the ridges of the gill pan or the hot grates of the grill to make a nonstick surface. Remove the shrimp from the marinade and season with salt and pepper. Lay the shrimp on the hot grill and cook for 4 minutes on each side, until charred and firm.

To serve, combine the black-eyed peas, shredded ham hock meat, green onions, tomatoes, sliced jalapeño, and most of the rest of the cilantro in a large salad bowl. Throw in the grilled shrimp and the remaining vinaigrette and toss it all together. Taste and season with salt and pepper, and garnish with the remaining cilantro.

NOTE | To butterfly shrimp, cut lengthwise along the top of the shrimp, almost all the way through the other side. Then open the shrimp like a book, to lie flat.

Extra-virgin olive oil

3 garlic cloves, whacked with the flat side of a knife

1 jalapeño chile, halved

1 pound dried black-eyed peas, picked through and rinsed

2 smoked ham hocks (about 2 pounds total)

2 bay leaves

Kosher salt and freshly ground black pepper

1 recipe Citrus-Chile Vinaigrette (page 32)

3 pounds extra-large shrimp, peeled and butterflied (see Note)

2 tablespoons Ancho Chili Powder (page 29)

¼ cup extra-virgin olive oil

Juice of ½ lime

2½ large handfuls of fresh cilantro, chopped

1 bunch of green onions, white and green parts, chopped

3 ripe tomatoes, chopped

1 jalapeño, thinly sliced

Kosher salt and freshly ground black pepper

Grilled Fat Pieces of Squid

45 minutes | Serves 4

This is a great summer fish salad full of brilliant Thai flavors. It's hard to believe so much flavor can come out of a dressing so simple—chile paste, honey, fresh lime juice—tossed with grilled squid and a bit of mint. Dynamite.

If you're using wooden skewers, soak them in water for 20 minutes before using them so that they don't catch fire on the grill.

Place a large grill pan on two burners over medium-high heat or preheat an outdoor gas or charcoal grill and get it very hot. Take a few paper towels and fold them several times to make a square. Blot a small amount of oil on the paper towels and then carefully and quickly wipe the hot grates of the grill (or the ridges of the grill pan) to create a nonstick surface.

Rinse the squid under cool water and pat dry. Split the tubes from top to bottom, then cut in half diagonally so that you get 2 triangles from each squid. Score the flesh lightly in a diamond pattern. Thread a skewer through the length of each to keep the squid flat on the grill. Toss with olive oil and sprinkle with salt and pepper. Lay the calamari on the grill and cook for 2 minutes on each side.

Serve the squid with the chili sauce, along with lime juice and mint leaves.

2 pounds squid bodies and tentacles, cleaned

Extra-virgin olive oil

Kosher salt and freshly ground black pepper

1 recipe Sweet Chili Sauce with Lime (page 32)

Juice of 1 lime

Fresh mint leaves, for serving

Herb-Seared Tuna with Caponata

About 1 ¼ hours | Serves 4

Classic Sicilian caponata is an eggplant dish that is traditionally seved as an accompaniment to fish or eaten on its own, as an appetizer, with bread. The flavors hit your tongue in a few different places. It's spicy from chiles, bright from the balsamic vinegar, salty with olives and capers, and sweet with raisins. Served at room temperature with all the ingredients melting into one taste, it's delicious with a piece of tuna.

CAPONATA

1 cup extra-virgin olive oil

6 anchovy fillets, coarsely chopped

2 teaspoons dried red pepper flakes

6 to 8 medium Japanese or 2 large Italian eggplants (1 ½ to 2 pounds total), cubed

4 tomatoes, halved, seeds squeezed out, coarsely chopped

2 red bell peppers, chopped

2 medium onions, diced

6 garlic cloves, minced

6 tablespoons capers, drained

½ cup raisins

1 cup pitted kalamata olives

¼ cup balsamic vinegar

Pinch of sugar

Leaves from 1 bunch of fresh basil, torn into pieces by hand

Kosher salt and freshly ground black pepper

LEMON CRÈME FRAÎCHE SAUCE

4 cups chicken stock, homemade (see page 36) or store-bought

2 garlic cloves

Zest of 2 lemons, finely grated

½ cup crème fraîche

To make the caponata, pour the oil into a large, deep skillet and put that over medium heat. Add the anchovies and red pepper flakes and cook and stir for a few minutes to create a flavor base. Turn off the heat and let the flavors infuse into the oil for a few minutes. Then turn the heat up to medium-high. Add the eggplants and fry them in this infused oil, stirring often, until they get brown and sticky, 3 to 5 minutes. Add the tomatoes, red bell peppers, onions, and garlic and continue to cook, stirring every now and then, until the vegetables break down and soften, about 15 more minutes. Throw in the capers, raisins, olives, balsamic vinegar, sugar, and basil. Lower the heat and simmer slowly until thickened, 30 to 35 minutes. Season with salt and pepper and set aside. (The caponata tastes great hot, cold, or at room temperature.)

In the meantime, make the sauce. Put the chicken stock, garlic, and lemon zest in a saucepan and place over medium heat. Simmer gently until the stock is reduced by half and thickened slightly. Take the pot off the heat, fish out the garlic, and stir in the crème fraîche. Set that aside, too.

Now move on to the tuna. Rub a little olive oil on the tuna. Put the chopped herbs in a flat dish, season with salt and pepper, and roll the tuna in the seasoned herbs to coat all over (don't get rid of the herbs; you'll use them to finish the caponata). Place 2 large skillets over medium-high heat and drizzle each with a 2-count of olive oil. When the oil gets hazy, lay the herb-coated tuna in the hot pans and sear for approximately 2 minutes on each side. As the tuna cooks, you'll see the red meat begin to whiten; you want the center of the tuna to remain rare and red. Transfer the tuna to a cutting board and slice about ½ inch thick.

Just before you are ready to plate the dish, buzz the sauce with a hand-held blender until it's thick and frothy. Taste the caponata and throw in a little of the seasoned herb mixture left over from the tuna.

Spoon the caponata onto four plates, lay the herb-seared tuna slices around the center, and drizzle the whole thing with the frothy lemon crème fraîche sauce.

TUNA

Extra-virgin olive oil

2 1-pound hunks of sushi-quality tuna, 1 1/2 inches thick

2 cups chopped fresh herbs, such as basil, flat-leaf parsley, and chives

Kosher salt and freshly ground black pepper

Salmon Salad with Green Herb Dressing and Couscous

1 hour | Serves 4 to 6

This is a summer crowd-pleaser. It looks beautiful on a platter and it's quick, healthy, and tasty. It's great with a glass of Sauvignon Blanc.

Preheat the oven to 250°F. Put the salmon in a baking dish, sprinkle with salt and pepper, drizzle with a 2-count of olive oil, and bake until just barely cooked through (the salmon should still be pinkish in the center), about 25 minutes.

Put the couscous into a medium bowl. Pour the water over it and stir with a fork to combine. Cover with foil or plastic wrap and let it sit for 10 to 15 minutes, then uncover and fluff with a fork. In the meantime, melt the butter in a large sauté pan over medium heat. Add the fennel, currants, shallots, and lemon slices and juice to the pan and let that all soften for 5 minutes, stirring occasionally. Toss into a large mixing bowl and season with salt and pepper. Fold in the couscous. Break the salmon into pieces and fold it into the couscous along with enough of the mayonnaise to moisten it. Serve at room temperature topped with chopped fennel fronds.

2 pounds center-cut salmon fillet

Kosher salt and freshly ground black pepper

Extra-virgin olive oil

2 cups couscous (12 ounces)

3 cups cold water

2 tablespoons unsalted butter

1 fennel bulb, trimmed and cut into thin strips, fronds reserved

1/4 cup currants

2 shallots, minced

1/2 lemon, sliced paper-thin and seeded

Juice of 1/2 lemon

Kosher salt and freshly ground black pepper

1/2 recipe Mayonnaise with a Fistful of Herbs (page 16)

Barcelona-Style Rice

1 ¼ hours + 30 minutes to marinate the chicken I Serves 4

There's a restaurant in Barcelona off La Ramblas—the "walking district"—called Las Turcoles, which means charcoal. You walk down an unassuming cobblestone street and into an even more unassuming bar. To get to the restaurant you walk through the kitchen where there are fifteen Spaniards standing around a train-engine of a coal-fed stove. The place looks and smells like Spain at its finest: paprika, chorizo, hams, and garlic.

I knew I was in the right place when I got to the bottom of my dish. The rice was toasted and crunchy, like a perfect paella should be. Using a method called *socarrat,* the chefs crank up the heat under the rice really high once it's cooked through, until they smell the rice begin to toast, and then shut it off. It was one of the most delicious things I've ever tasted.

2 chicken thighs

2 chicken legs

1 teaspoon dried oregano

2 tablespoons sweet paprika

Kosher salt and freshly ground black pepper

¼ cup extra-virgin olive oil

1 Spanish chorizo sausage

4 garlic cloves, crushed

1 onion, diced

1 (14-ounce) can whole, peeled tomatoes, drained and hand crushed

1 cup Spanish rice, short to medium grain

1 teaspoon saffron threads

4 jumbo shrimp, peeled

2 lobster tails, split

6 littleneck clams, scrubbed

½ cup frozen sweet peas, thawed

Fresh flat-leaf parsley leaves, for garnish

Lemon wedges, for serving

Rinse the chicken pieces and pat dry. Mix the oregano and paprika with some salt and pepper in a small bowl. Rub the spice mixture all over the chicken and stick it in the refrigerator to marinate for 30 minutes.

Heat the oil in a paella pan or wide shallow skillet over medium-high heat. When the oil is beginning to smoke, add the chicken, skin side down, and brown all over, turning with tongs. Add the chorizo and continue to cook until the oil is a vibrant red color. Remove the chicken and sausage to a platter lined with paper towels.

Return the pan to the stove and lower the heat to medium. Now make a sofrito by sautéing the garlic and onion in the oil that remains in the pan for 7 to 10 minutes, until they begin to brown. Add the tomatoes and cook it all down until the mixture caramelizes a bit and the flavors meld. Season with salt and pepper. Fold in the rice, stirring to coat the grains. Stir in the saffron. Pour in 3 cups warm water and simmer for 10 minutes, gently moving the pan around so the rice cooks evenly and absorbs the liquid. Do not cover or stir constantly as you would a risotto.

Add the shrimp, lobster, clams, and the reserved chicken and chorizo. Give the paella a couple of good stirs to tuck all the pieces in there, then just let it simmer, without stirring, until the rice is al dente, about 15 minutes. Scatter the peas on top and continue to cook for 5 more minutes, until the paella looks fluffy and moist. (The ideal paella has a toasted rice bottom called socarrat.) Then let it rest off the heat for 5 minutes. Garnish with parsley and serve with lemon wedges.

Argentinian Gaucho Steak

40 minutes | Serves 6 to 8

If skirt steak, which is traditionally used for this Argentinian recipe, is difficult to get your hands on, flank steak is a great substite. The chimichurri sauce is a great condiment for any kind of roasted or grilled meat. In the summer, I'll make a batch of this stuff and just leave it in the refrigerator. It's excellent with roasted lamb.

CHIMICHURRI SAUCE

6 garlic cloves, minced

Kosher salt

1 jalapeño, minced

¼ cup red wine vinegar

1 bunch of fresh flat-leaf parsley, chopped

2 handfuls of fresh oregano, finely chopped

Juice of 2 limes

1 cup extra-virgin olive oil

1 teaspoon crushed black peppercorns

Extra-virgin olive oil

4 pounds skirt steak, trimmed of excess fat

Kosher salt and freshly ground black pepper

Thick slices of Tuscan bread

Campfire Roasted Red Peppers (recipe follows)

Salsa Criolla (recipe follows)

Combine the garlic and the salt on a cutting board and grind together to a paste with the back of a chef's knife. Put the paste into a bowl and stir in the jalapeño, vinegar, parsley, oregano, and lime juice. Whisk in the olive oil and season with salt and the crushed peppercorns. Set aside at room temperature to allow the flavors to marry.

Place a large grill pan on two burners over medium-high heat or preheat an outdoor gas or charcoal grill and get it very hot (you can also use a broiler). Take a few paper towels and fold them several times to make a thick square. Blot a small amount of oil on the paper towels. Then carefully and quickly wipe the hot grates of the grill to make a nonstick grilling surface. Drizzle the steak with oil and season both sides with a generous amount of salt and pepper. You should actually see the seasoning on the meat. Grill the steaks on the grill pan or the hottest part of the grill for 4 minutes per side, or until well charred. Transfer the steaks to a cutting board and let them rest for 5 minutes. Brush the bread on both sides with oil and grill until marked and lightly toasted, about 2 minutes per side.

Cut the steak across the grain on an angle and fan the slices out on a platter. Spoon some chimichurri sauce over the meat. Serve with roasted red peppers, salsa criolla, the grilled bread, and the rest of the chimichurri sauce.

Campfire-Roasted Red Peppers

30 minutes | Serves 6

6 large red bell peppers | Extra-virgin olive oil | Kosher salt and freshly ground black pepper

Preheat an outdoor gas or charcoal grill to medium-high. Rub the red peppers with oil and season them with salt and pepper. Place the peppers directly on the grill and roast for 10 minutes, turning periodically with tongs, so they are really charred and blistered all over. Put the peppers into a bowl, cover with plastic wrap, and steam for about 10 minutes to loosen their skins. Pull out the cores of the red peppers and remove the seeds. Peel the blackened skins and tear the peppers into strips. Put them into a bowl and serve.

Salsa Criolla **30 minutes | Serves 6**

2 medium onions | 3 ripe tomatoes | 4 garlic cloves, minced | 2 handfuls of fresh flat-leaf parsley, chopped | Kosher salt and freshly ground black pepper | 3 tablespoons red wine vinegar | $1/2$ cup extra-virgin olive oil

Chop the onions and tomatoes into bite-size pieces and put into a bowl; add the garlic and parsley and season generously with salt and pepper. Pour in the vinegar and oil and mix well to incorporate the ingredients. Taste and adjust the seasonings as needed. Serve at room temperature.

Grilled Steak Salad with Peaches and Lime Dressing

1 hour + 1 hour marinating time | Serves 6

These are classic summer barbecue flavors. Grilling sweetens up the peaches and they get really juicy. I love grilling limes and lemons, too. The juices on the outside start to caramelize and get smoky; the caramelized lime juice is just delicious.

3 pounds skirt or flank steak, trimmed of excess fat

1 recipe Ancho Chili Powder (page 29)

Extra-virgin olive oil

6 ripe but firm peaches, halved and pitted

Kosher salt and freshly ground black pepper

2 limes, cut into $1/4$-inch-thick slices

4 cups micro greens or baby mixed greens

1 cup toasted pecans

First lay the steak out on a large platter or piece of plastic wrap and rub both sides with the chili powder. Put it in the refrigerator and let it marinate for about an hour so the flavors can really get into the meat.

While you're waiting, place a large grill pan on two burners over medium-high heat or preheat an outdoor gas or charcoal grill and get it very hot. Take a few paper towels and fold them several times to make a thick square. Blot a small amount of oil on the paper towels. Then carefully and quickly wipe the hot grates of the grill to make a nonstick grilling surface. Rub the peaches all over with oil and season with salt and pepper. Put the lime slices and peaches, cut side down, on the grill and cook for 5 to 8 minutes, until the flesh softens a little and caramelizes to bring out the sweetness of the fruit. Remove the limes to a platter. Turn the peaches over with tongs and grill the other side for 3 minutes to char the skin; put those on the platter, too.

Now you're ready to cook the steak. Rub it all over with oil and season both sides with salt and pepper. Put the steak on the grill pan or the hottest part of the grill so that it develops a good crust, and grill for 4 minutes per side, until well charred. Transfer to a cutting board and let it rest for about 5 minutes before slicing. (This will give the juices a chance to redistribute throughout the meat.) Cut the meat across the grain on an angle.

To assemble the salad, put the greens on a clean serving platter and arrange the peach halves, lime slices, and steak on top. Sprinkle with the pecans and drizzle with olive oil, and you're done.

Mexican Street Tacos

45 minutes + at least 1 hour to marinate the meat | Serves 4

The open-air market in Oaxaca is an eye-popping place. At one stall, a woman makes tacos like these, grilling the tortillas on what looks like half of an oil drum, cut out, with a fire underneath it. When they are hot, she fills them with stewed chicken in mole sauce, zucchini flowers, soft Mexican cheese, or grilled steak. If you could make a flavor out of putting your face in the sun and feeling the warmth on your cheek, this would be it.

Lay the flank steak in a large baking dish and pour the mojo over it. Wrap tightly in plastic wrap and refrigerate for 1 hour or up to 8 hours, so the flavors can sink into the meat. (Don't marinate the steak for more than 8 hours or the fibers will break down too much and the meat will get mushy.)

Preheat an outdoor grill or a ridged grill pan over a medium-high flame (you can also use your broiler). Take a few paper towels and fold them several times to make a thick square. Blot a small amount of oil on the towels, then carefully and quickly wipe the hot grates to make a nonstick grilling surface. Pull the steak out of the mojo marinade and season on both sides with salt and pepper. Grill (or broil) the steak for 7 to 10 minutes per side, turning once, until medium-rare. Remove to a cutting board and let it rest for 5 minutes to allow the juices to settle. Slice thin on an angle, across the grain.

While the steak is resting, warm the tortillas for 30 seconds on each side in a dry skillet or on the grill, until toasty and pliable. To serve, put two of the warm tortillas on your work surface. Lay about an eighth of the beef down the center of each, and sprinkle with lettuce, onion, and cheese. Top with a spoonful of pico de gallo and garnish with lime wedges. Repeat to make 6 more tacos.

Mojo — **Makes about 1 ¼ cups**

4 garlic cloves, minced | 2 jalapeños, minced | 1 large handful of fresh cilantro, finely chopped | Kosher salt and freshly ground black pepper | Juice of 2 limes | Juice of 2 oranges | 2 tablespoons white vinegar | ½ cup extra-virgin olive oil

With a mortar and pestle, mash together the garlic, jalapeños, cilantro, salt, and pepper to make a paste. Put it in a glass jar. Add the lime and orange juices, the vinegar, and the oil and shake it up to combine.

---

2 pounds flank or skirt steak, trimmed of excess fat
Mojo (recipe follows)
Olive oil, for coating the grill
Kosher salt and freshly ground black pepper
8 (7-inch) corn tortillas
Shredded romaine or iceberg lettuce
Chopped onion
Crumbled queso fresco or grated Monterey Jack cheese
1 recipe Pico de Gallo (page 96)
2 limes, cut into wedges

Chili Cheese Dogs

1 hour | Serves 4

At the end of the day, a good chili dog is still hard to beat. This recipe is my dad's, and to this day, it's the best hot dog I've ever tasted.

Extra-virgin olive oil

1 medium onion, chopped

1 pound lean ground beef

1 cup ketchup

1 teaspoon chili powder

2 teaspoons prepared yellow mustard

Kosher salt and freshly ground
  black pepper

4 all-beef hot dogs

4 hot dog rolls

$^1/_2$ cup grated Cheddar cheese

Put a skillet over medium heat and drizzle in a 2-count of olive oil. When the oil gets hazy, add the onion and cook, stirring, until it is soft and translucent, about 5 minutes. Add the ground beef, breaking it up with the back of a spoon, and cook until nicely browned, about 10 more minutes. Stir in the ketchup, chili powder, and mustard and simmer for 15 minutes, or until thickened. Season with salt and pepper.

While the chili is cooking, get the grill going. Place a large grill pan on two burners over medium-high heat or preheat an outdoor gas or charcoal grill and get it very hot. Take a few paper towels and fold them several times to make a thick square. Blot a small amount of oil on the paper towels. Then carefully and quickly wipe the hot grates of the grill to make a nonstick grilling surface.

Bring a pot of water up to a simmer and parboil the dogs for about 5 minutes. Take them out of the water, pat them dry, and grill them just long enough to mark them. (That'll give them a grilled flavor, too.) Brush the insides of the rolls with olive oil and lay them face down on the grill; cook until toasty. To serve, put a dog in each roll and top with the chili and some Cheddar cheese.

Tangerine-Glazed Ham with Baby Carrots

4¼ hours, baking time included | **Serves 8 to 10**

I wanted to do a cool, whole ham recipe for this book—an Easter project that'll make you look like a million dollars. The glaze for this thing sort of melts into the ham and forms a crackling crust. It's the best ham you'll ever taste.

Preheat the oven to 300°F. Put the ham in a large roasting pan, fat side up. Using a sharp knife, score the ham in a diamond pattern with cuts across the skin, about 2 inches apart and ½ inch deep. Season the meat generously with salt and pepper. Chop about 8 of the sage leaves and stir that up with the oil to make a paste. Rub the paste all over the ham, being sure to get the flavor into all the cuts. Put the ham in the oven; you're going to bake it for about 4 hours total, but you'll need to glaze it at 3 hours. This gives you plenty of time to bang out the tangerine glaze.

Put a saucepan over medium heat. Add the chunks of butter, tangerines, tangerine juice, brown sugar, 1 cup of water, and the spices. Bring to a simmer, then slowly cook the liquid down to a syrupy glaze. This should take 30 to 40 minutes.

After the ham has been going for 3 hours, take the pan out of the oven and carefully spoon out as much of the fat as you can; discard. Scatter the carrots around the ham. Pour the tangerine glaze, with the pieces of fruit, all over the ham and carrots. Scatter the remaining sage leaves on top, stick the ham back in the oven, and continue to cook for 1 more hour, basting with the juices after 30 minutes, until the carrots are tender, the ham is dark and crispy, and the whole thing is glistening with a sweet glaze.

Set the ham on a cutting board to rest for about 10 minutes before carving. Serve the carrots with the tangerine glaze on the side.

1 (8- to 10-pound) fresh smoked ham, bone in, skin on

Kosher salt and freshly ground black pepper

1 bunch of fresh sage leaves

¼ cup extra-virgin olive oil

1 cup (2 sticks) unsalted butter, cut into chunks

2 tangerines, sliced thin (with the peel), seeds removed

2 cups tangerine juice

2 cups packed light brown sugar

¼ teaspoon whole cloves

2 cinnamon sticks

1½ pounds young carrots (about 6 inches long), tops trimmed

Grilled Rack of Lamb with Garden Purée and Mint

1 ¹/₂ hours, including marinating the lamb | Serves 6

This garden purée wraps its flavors around the lamb. Asparagus, green beans, and sweet peas at the peak of freshness are puréed together with rich whole-milk ricotta cheese. It's lush. It's incredibly delicious by itself; you're going to have a hard time keeping your spoon out of it. But with the grilled rack of lamb and a warm summer breeze, you'll know absolutely what time of year it is.

2 lamb racks (about 2 pounds each,
   7 or 8 ribs apiece), trimmed
   and Frenched
Extra-virgin olive oil
1 lemon, sliced paper-thin
Leaves from ¹/₂ bunch of fresh mint,
   shredded
Leaves from ¹/₂ bunch of fresh
   oregano
Kosher salt and freshly ground
   black pepper

GARDEN PURÉE

Kosher salt and freshly ground
   black pepper
¹/₂ pound sugar snap peas, trimmed
1 pound English peas, shelled, or
   1 cup frozen petite peas
¹/₂ pound asparagus, tips only
   (about 2¹/₂ inches)
¹/₂ pound haricots verts or tender
   green beans, trimmed
²/₃ cup whole-milk ricotta cheese
3 green onions, green parts only,
   roughly chopped
Extra-virgin olive oil

1 bunch of green onions, trimmed
Fresh mint leaves, for garnish

Put the lamb in a baking dish and drizzle with ¹/₄ cup of olive oil. Add the lemon slices, mint, oregano, and salt and pepper and turn the lamb in the mixture to coat. Stick it in the refrigerator to marinate for 1 hour.

Bring a large pot of salted water to a boil. Add the peas, asparagus tips, and haricots verts and cook until bright green and crisp-tender, about 3 minutes. (If you're using frozen peas, you can throw them in during the last couple of minutes, to thaw.) Drain, transfer to a bowl of salted ice water to stop the cooking, and drain again. Purée in a food processor with the ricotta, green onion greens, a drizzle of oil, and salt and pepper to taste. Scrape that out into a medium saucepan and set it aside while you cook the lamb.

Preheat an outdoor gas or charcoal grill or a ridged grill pan over a medium-high flame. Take a few paper towels and fold them several times to make a thick square. Blot a small amount of oil on the paper towels. Then carefully and quickly wipe the hot grates of the grill to make a nonstick grilling surface. Put the lamb on the hottest part of the grill and cook, turning once, until medium-rare, 12 to 15 minutes. Remove to a cutting board and let rest for 10 minutes to allow the juices to redistribute throughout the meat. Toss the whole green onions in oil, sprinkle with salt and pepper, and grill, turning once, until marked and barely softened, about 2 minutes.

To serve, warm the purée over low heat. Cut the racks into double chops and serve with the garden purée and the green onions, garnished with mint leaves.

Pulled Pork Barbecue

6 $\frac{1}{2}$ hours including roasting + marinating | Serves 12

DRY RUB

3 tablespoons paprika

1 tablespoon garlic powder

1 tablespoon brown sugar

1 tablespoon dry mustard

3 tablespoons coarse sea salt

1 (5- to 7-pound) pork roast,
preferably shoulder or Boston butt

CIDER-VINEGAR BARBECUE
SAUCE

1 $\frac{1}{2}$ cups cider vinegar

1 cup yellow or brown mustard

$\frac{1}{2}$ cup ketchup

$\frac{1}{3}$ cup brown sugar

2 garlic cloves, smashed

1 teaspoon kosher salt

1 teaspoon cayenne pepper

$\frac{1}{2}$ teaspoon freshly ground
black pepper

12 hamburger buns

Spicy Slaw (recipe follows)

Pickle spears

Mix the paprika, garlic powder, brown sugar, dry mustard, and sea salt together in a small bowl. Rub the spice blend all over the pork and marinate for as long as you have time for—as little as 1 hour, or up to overnight (refrigerate it, covered).

Preheat the oven to 300°F. Put the pork in a roasting pan and roast it for about 6 hours. An instant-read thermometer stuck into the thickest part of the pork should register 170°F., but basically, what you want to do is roast it until it's falling apart.

While the pork is going, make the barbecue sauce. Combine the vinegar, mustard, ketchup, brown sugar, garlic, kosher salt, cayenne pepper, and black pepper in a saucepan over medium heat. Simmer gently, stirring, for 10 minutes, or until the sugar dissolves. Take it off the heat and let it sit until you're ready for it.

When the pork is done, take it out of the oven and put it on a large platter. Allow the meat to rest for about 10 minutes. Then while it's still warm, you want to "pull" the meat: Grab two forks. Using one to steady the meat, use the other to "pull" shreds of meat off the roast. Put the shredded pork in a bowl and pour half of the sauce over. Stir it all up well so that the pork is coated with the sauce.

To serve, spoon the pulled pork mixture onto the bottom half of each hamburger bun, and top with some slaw. Serve with pickle spears and the remaining sauce on the side.

Spicy Slaw   **30 minutes + chilling time | Makes 8 to 10 cups**

1 head of green cabbage, shredded | 2 carrots, grated | 1 red onion, thinly sliced | 2 green onions (white and green parts), chopped | 1 fresh red chile, sliced | 1 $\frac{1}{2}$ cups mayonnaise | $\frac{1}{4}$ cup Dijon mustard | 1 tablespoon cider vinegar | Juice of 1 lemon | Pinch of sugar | $\frac{1}{2}$ teaspoon celery seed | Several dashes of hot sauce | Kosher salt and freshly ground black pepper

Combine the cabbage, carrots, red onion, green onions, and chile in a large bowl. In another bowl, mix the mayonnaise, mustard, vinegar, lemon juice, and sugar and stir it all up to blend. Pour the dressing over the cabbage mixture and toss gently to mix. Season the cole slaw with celery seed, hot sauce, salt, and black pepper. Chill for 2 hours in the refrigerator before serving.

Raw Bar

JUST THINKING ABOUT A RAW BAR IN THE SUMMER MAKES ME HUNGRY AND SMILE. THERE'S SOMETHING ABOUT THE TASTE OF FRESHLY SHUCKED SHELLFISH—IT'S BRINY AND SOFT, LIKE BUTTER AND COOL, GREEN SEAWATER. I LOVE PUTTING TOGETHER RAW BARS. They add an instant elegant-cool factor to any impromptu get-together. The sauces in this chapter will also make you shine. There's everything from a Japanese twist on a mignonette to a classic cocktail sauce. It'll taste like having a beach in your backyard.

The techniques for opening raw clams and oysters are a little different but the process starts out the same. First thing is, buy shellfish that is impeccably fresh—that means it smells great, the shells aren't broken, and the shells are tightly closed. Discard any that open between the time you buy them and get home. Hold them on ice (not in water) in the refrigerator until you're ready to shuck and eat them. And plan on eating as quickly as you can shuck.

Scrub both oysters and clams under cold water with a stiff brush to get rid of all the dirt. Next, get yourself a shellfish glove—or a heavyweight cloth will work—to steady the shellfish as you're shucking and also protect your hand from any wayward jabs of the knife. If you're using a cloth, fold it over several times into a square to make a mitt.

TO SHUCK OYSTERS Hold the oyster firmly in the palm of your towel- or glove-covered hand with the fatter side up. Have a bowl nearby to collect the juices. Insert the tip of an oyster knife between the shell halves at the hinge; work it around one side to the other as you pry it open. Once the shell has opened a bit, you can run the knife along the inside of the top shell to cut the adductor muscle away from that shell, bend the shell back to release it, and discard. Then slide the knife underneath the oyster to detach it completely, but leave it in its shell (take care not to cut the meat itself). Tip the juice out into the bowl so you can pick out any bits of shell, then pour it back over the shucked oysters.

TO SHUCK CLAMS You're going to use a clam knife, which is the same size as an oyster knife, but one side is honed to a dull edge. Look carefully at a clam—you'll see that one side of the shell (to the right or left of the hinge) is fatter than the other. Hold the clam in your glove- or mitt-covered hand with the thin side in your palm and the chubby side sticking up. Wedge the blade side of the knife into the seam between the shells and press and work it until you can get between the shells. Then continue on just as for oysters.

Raw Oysters and Clams on the Half Shell
As quick as you can shuck! I **Makes 24 oysters**

24 oysters, such as Malpèque, Wellfleet, Kumamoto, Blue Point, or Belon, scrubbed and shucked (see page 192) I 24 littleneck clams, scrubbed and shucked (see page 192) I Crushed ice or rock salt I Cocktail Sauce (the Classic) (recipe follows) I Japanese Mignonette (recipe follows) I Mango-Radish Salsa (page 196)

Nestle the oysters and clams in a bed of crushed ice or rock salt to keep them steady. Serve with one or all three of the sauces.

Cocktail Sauce (the Classic)
15 minutes + about 1 hour to chill I Makes about ³⁄₄ cup

Cocktail sauce is one of those tastes you can't stop eating. I don't care if it is just ketchup and horseradish—I could eat a whole bowl of this stuff.

¹⁄₂ cup ketchup I ¹⁄₄ cup grated fresh or prepared horseradish I Juice of 1 lemon I 1 tablespoon Worcestershire sauce I A few drops of hot pepper sauce

Stir together all of the ingredients in a bowl and chill for about 1 hour to allow the flavors to come together.

Japanese Mignonette

20 minutes + at least 1 hour to chill | Makes 1 cup

A classic mignonette is made of vinegar, shallots, and black pepper. The cucumber in this recipe heightens the taste of the shellfish. (When you put salt on cucumber, it tastes kind of oceany anyway.) Shiso tastes like a lemony mint and it's delicious with the cucumber. I get my shiso from a local sushi place on the way home.

1 cup rice vinegar | 1 shallot, minced | 1-inch piece of fresh ginger, peeled and grated | $^1/_2$ hothouse cucumber, peeled and minced | Several turns of freshly ground black pepper | 1 handful of fresh cilantro, chopped | 2 shiso leaves, cut into chiffonade (optional)

In a small bowl, combine the rice vinegar, shallot, ginger, cucumber, black pepper, and cilantro. Mix it all up with a fork. Cover and chill for at least 1 hour or up to 24 hours before you plan to serve, to allow the flavors to come together. Stir in the shiso just before serving, if using.

Mango-Radish Salsa 30 minutes | Makes about 1 ¹/₂ cups

This is one of my favorite pairings for shellfish, particularly clams, because the briny flavor of the clams tastes just delicious with the mangos.

2 limes | 2 mangos, peeled and finely diced | 4 to 5 red radishes, finely diced | 1 tablespoon chili powder | ¹/₂ bunch of fresh cilantro, chopped (about ¹/₄ cup) | ¹/₄ cup extra-virgin olive oil | Kosher salt and freshly ground black pepper

Cut off the top and bottom ends of the limes so that they stand upright. Then use a knife to cut off the peel in long strips, including as much of the bitter white pith as possible. Working over a bowl to catch the juices, cut between the membranes to free the lime sections; seed them and drop them into the bowl. Discard the membranes. Add all of the rest of the ingredients and stir gently.

Steamed Lobster with Lemon-Caper Mayonnaise

30 minutes + about 2 hours to chill | Serves 4

When I was fifteen years old, I started washing dishes in the coolest restaurant in my hometown. One of my jobs was to cook and break down the lobsters for the evening service. Tasting the salty lobster with fresh, rich mayonnaise was, without question, my first food epiphany.

Steaming is my favorite way to cook lobster; it condenses the lobster flavor and keeps the meat moist. When you boil, you extract flavor, so that the water tastes like lobster but the lobster tastes bland.

Put about 2 inches of water in a large steamer or soup pot. Add the salt and squeeze in the lemon juice; toss the halves in there, too, for extra flavor. Bring to a boil over medium heat.

Place the lobsters in the steamer basket or directly in the pot, cover, and steam until they turn bright red, about 15 minutes. Remove the lobsters from the pot and drain. Cool them to room temperature, then chill thoroughly before you crack them open. Serve with lemon wedges and Lemon-Caper Mayonnaise.

1 tablespoon kosher salt

2 lemons, halved, plus more for
  serving

4 (1 1/2-pound) live lobsters

Lemon-Caper Mayonnaise (page 19)

Shrimp Poached with Beer, Old Bay, and Lemon

20 minutes + at least 1 hour for chilling | Serves 4

Nothing makes a crowd happier on a warm night than dumping a pot of freshly poached shrimp on a picnic table covered with newspapers, with a bucket of cold beer and lots of towels to wipe your hands on.

Fill a large pot with about 2 quarts of water. Crack open the beer and pour that in. Add the salt and squeeze in the lemon juice; toss the halves in, too. Add the herbs, the garlic, and the Old Bay. Bring to a boil over medium-high heat and simmer for 5 minutes to infuse the water with the aromatics.

Now reduce the heat to medium-low and put the shrimp in there. Simmer, uncovered, for 2 to 3 minutes, or until the shrimp are bright pink. Drain, then transfer to a bowl. Chill thoroughly, then peel. Serve with lemon wedges and cocktail sauce.

1 bottle of beer (any kind you like)

2 teaspoons kosher salt

2 lemons, halved

3 bay leaves

1 handful of fresh thyme sprigs

1 head of garlic, split horizontally

1 tablespoon Old Bay Seasoning

2 pounds jumbo shrimp, with shells,
  heads, and tails

Lemon wedges, for serving

1 recipe Cocktail Sauce (the Classic)
  (page 194)

SAVORING

I had a crazy schedule last year, but I managed to get a two-week break right before the holidays. It was truly one of the happiest times I can remember. It was my son and me, hanging out at home every day in my apartment in New York City, **LAUGHING AND COOKING**, shopping, writing recipes, and watching cartoons.

I remember one day closing my eyes for a second and **PAUSING TO SMELL** the apartment. A fresh, homemade turkey stock was simmering on the stove for a roasted pumpkin soup; a big casserole of lamb shanks had been braising for hours in the oven in red wine and cinnamon. **THE WHOLE PLACE SMELLED WARM AND INVITING**—I was so glad to be home—and I realized how important it was to **SAVOR THE IMPORTANT STUFF**.

Thai Chicken Soup

30 minutes | Serves 4 to 6

I love spicy food in the winter. It warms you up from the inside. I started experimenting with the flavors of Thailand about ten years ago. Thai food has become as global as sushi. You can go to any major city in the country and find a great Thai restaurant. This classic soup is a great example of how truly mind-blowing Thai flavors are. They hit your tongue in so many different places: sour, spicy, salty, and sweet, all at the same time. When the weather's cold, this is the soup I crave.

In a soup pot, bring the stock to a boil over medium heat. Add the lemongrass, Kaffir lime leaves, ginger, chiles, and garlic. Reduce the heat and simmer, covered, for 10 minutes to let the spices infuse the broth.

Uncover and stir in the coconut milk, fish sauce, sugar, mushrooms, shredded chicken, lime juice, and cracked pepper to taste. Cook for 5 minutes to heat the chicken through. Ladle the soup into a soup tureen or individual serving bowls and garnish with the cilantro. (When you serve the soup, try to leave the lemongrass, ginger, and lime leaves in the pot.)

1 quart chicken stock, homemade (see page 36) or store-bought

1 lemongrass stalk, white part only, crushed and opened with the flat side of a knife

3 Kaffir lime leaves, fresh or dried, hand torn

3-inch piece of fresh ginger, peeled and sliced

2 small fresh Thai bird chiles, halved lengthwise

2 garlic cloves, peeled and smashed

1 (13- to 14-ounce) can unsweetened coconut milk

2 tablespoons Thai fish sauce (nam pla)

1 $\frac{1}{2}$ teaspoons sugar

1 (8-ounce) can straw mushrooms, rinsed and halved

1 $\frac{1}{2}$ cups shredded cooked chicken (see page 37)

Juice of 4 limes

Fresh cracked black pepper

$\frac{1}{4}$ cup chopped fresh cilantro

Tyler's Manhattan Clam Chowder

1 ¼ hours | Serves 6

During one of the episodes of *Tyler's Ultimate,* I got to hang out with Jasper White. He's one of the most talented chefs in the country, a true Bostonian institution but also a national treasure. I picked up more from him in one afternoon about how to make a proper New England chowder than I'd learned in all my years cooking up until then. But here's the deal: I live in Manhattan. So here's my answer to Jasper's delicious New England clam chowder. He can come to my house any time.

3 tablespoons unsalted butter

1 large onion, roughly chopped

2 celery stalks, roughly chopped

4 garlic cloves, chopped

1 chorizo sausage link, sliced into ½-inch rounds

1 tablespoon all-purpose flour

1 recipe Clam Broth with Bacon and Fresh Thyme (page 36)

8 medium tomatoes, seeded (see Note) and puréed in a food processor

1 tablespoon sugar

1 tablespoon dried red pepper flakes

2 sprigs of fresh thyme

½ bunch of fresh flat-leaf parsley, chopped

Kosher salt and freshly ground black pepper

2 Idaho potatoes, peeled and cut into small cubes

2 dozen littleneck clams, scrubbed and soaked in cold water to remove dirt

In a large saucepot, melt the butter over medium heat. Toss in the onion, celery, garlic, and chorizo and cook for 4 to 5 minutes, or until the onion has wilted and is translucent. Stir in the flour to make a smooth paste. Slowly pour in the clam broth (with the chopped clams) and whisk or stir until smooth. Add the tomatoes and sugar and give it all a good stir. Toss in the pepper flakes, thyme, and parsley. Season with salt and pepper. Add the potatoes, bring to a boil, and boil hard for about 5 minutes. This will break down the potatoes and thicken up the soup. Then reduce the heat, cover, and simmer for 10 to 15 minutes, until the soup has reduced a little, the tomato has mellowed, and the flavors have come together.

Now toss in the littlenecks, cover, and simmer until the clams open, about 8 minutes. Discard any clams that didn't open. Stir the soup well, season it again if it needs it, and serve immediately.

NOTE | To seed tomatoes, cut them in half through the equator. Then, holding each half in the palm of your hand, cut side down, squeeze over the sink to get rid of the seeds.

WHEN THE WEATHER STARTS TO COOL AND AUTUMN IS IN FULL SWING, MY PALATE GRAVITATES TOWARD DEEP, SATISFYING FLAVORS—PUMPKINS AND PANCETTA, LAMB SHANKS BRAISED IN RED WINE WITH CREAMY POLENTA. I PULL MY PALATE'S WINTER WARDROBE OUT OF THE CLOSET.

Brothy Pumpkin Soup with Pancetta and Cabbage

2 hours + several hours to chill stock | Serves 8

The stock for this soup is made from rich, smoked turkey wings. It's easy to find them in grocery stores and they make the most savory broth you've ever tasted. The pumpkin is roasted in the oven until it falls apart with a spoon. The soup is rich and delicious and tastes great on a cold night. I use green-skinned Kabuki pumpkin for this because it's gorgeous and you don't need to peel it. You can use standard pumpkin or butternut squash; just peel it before you roast it.

Start by making the turkey broth. In a large stockpot, combine the turkey wings, onions, carrots, garlic, rutabaga, celery, bay leaves, and 1 gallon of cold water (or enough to cover by at least 3 inches). Bring the water to a boil, reduce the heat, and simmer for 45 minutes, skimming when you feel like it to remove any impurities that float to the top. Remove from the heat and strain into a large pot or bowl, pressing on the vegetables and meat to extract as much flavor as possible. Discard the vegetables, turkey, and herbs. Cool the broth to room temperature before storing in the refrigerator, or chill it down over ice first. When chilled, skim the surface again for any additional impurities. This can be done up to 3 days in advance.

Preheat the oven to 375°F. Toss the pumpkin in a large mixing bowl with the olive oil, nutmeg, minced sage, salt, and lots of pepper. Dump the pumpkin onto a baking sheet, spread it out in a single layer, and roast for 45 minutes or until very tender.

Now that you have all the elements, you can put the soup together. Put a large stockpot over medium-low heat. Add the pancetta and cook for 2 to 3 minutes to render out some of that delicious fat. Toss in the minced onion and garlic and cook for 2 minutes, or until the onion is translucent. Add the halved sage leaves and the cabbage and cook, stirring, for 3 to 5 minutes, or until the cabbage is wilted. Pour the strained, cooled broth into the pot and bring to a gentle simmer. Taste the soup and then season with salt and pepper. Ladle the soup into bowls and garnish with several pieces of pumpkin and a drizzle of olive oil.

BROTH

2 pounds smoked turkey wings

2 onions, quartered

2 carrots, roughly chopped

1/2 head of garlic

1 pound rutabaga, peeled and roughly chopped

2 celery stalks, roughly chopped

2 bay leaves

1 pumpkin or 2 medium butternut squash (5 pounds total), split, seeded, peeled, and cut into 2-inch pieces

1/4 cup extra-virgin olive oil, plus more for drizzling

1/2 teaspoon freshly grated nutmeg

2 tablespoons minced fresh sage plus 6 whole leaves, cut in half

Kosher salt and freshly ground black pepper

1 pound pancetta, cut into 1-inch pieces

1 onion, minced

3 garlic cloves, minced

2 small heads napa cabbage, thinly sliced

Pan-Roasted Chicken with Porcini Mushrooms, Prosciutto, and Marsala Sauce

45 minutes | Serves 4

4 skinless, boneless chicken breasts
   (about 1 ½ pounds total)

¾ cup all-purpose flour, for dredging

Kosher salt and freshly ground
   black pepper

¼ cup extra-virgin olive oil

4 ounces thinly sliced prosciutto,
   cut into ribbons

8 ounces fresh porcini or cremini
   mushrooms (or whatever
   mushrooms you find in your
   supermarket), wiped clean,
   stemmed, and halved

½ cup sweet Marsala wine

½ cup chicken stock, homemade
   (see page 36) or store-bought

2 tablespoons unsalted butter

¼ cup chopped fresh flat-leaf parsley

Put the chicken breasts side by side on a cutting board and lay a piece of plastic wrap over them. Pound to about ½ inch thick with a flat meat mallet, a heavy-bottomed saucepan, or a bottle. Put the flour in a shallow platter and season with a fair amount of salt and pepper. Mix with your fingers to incorporate the seasoning and then taste to make sure it's well seasoned.

Heat the oil over medium-high heat in a large skillet. When the oil is nice and hot, dredge the chicken cutlets in the seasoned flour and shake off the excess. Slip the cutlets into the pan and fry for 5 to 7 minutes on each side, until golden, turning once. (Do this in batches if the cutlets don't fit comfortably in the pan.) Remove the chicken to a large platter (arranging it in a single layer) and cover with foil to keep warm.

Now you're going to make a quick sauce. Lower the heat to medium and add the prosciutto to the pan. Add a drizzle of olive oil (about 2 teaspoons) and sauté for about 1 minute to render out some of the delicious fat. Add the mushrooms and another drizzle of oil and sauté until the mushrooms are nicely browned and their moisture has evaporated, about 5 minutes. Season with salt and pepper. Pour the Marsala into the pan and boil down for a few seconds to cook out the alcohol. Then add the chicken stock and simmer for a minute to reduce the sauce slightly. Stir in the butter and return the chicken to the pan. Simmer gently for 1 minute to heat the chicken through. Season with salt and pepper and garnish with chopped parsley before serving.

Roasted Leg of Lamb with Soft Fennel and Romesco Sauce

2 hours | Serves 8

In my travels in France, I used to shop at the farmers' market in the town of Valbon in Provence. The spice guy had all these amazing spices lined up and he'd make special blends if you gave him an idea what you were cooking. For lamb he put together this mixture (Turkish flavors, he said) and it tastes just unbelievable. Combinations like these are a pure example of the global palate, using ingredients that have been making their way around the globe for centuries.

Stir together the garlic, parsley, olive oil, salt, and pepper to make a paste. Spread that over the inside of the leg of lamb. Tie the leg crosswise with several lengths of butcher's twine. Coat the outside of the leg of lamb with the Turkish Spice Mix and set it on a rack in a roasting pan.

Preheat the oven to 375°F. Put the fennel in a small, deep baking dish (or soufflé dish) and sprinkle with salt and pepper. Add the lemon juice and enough oil to entirely cover the fennel ($2^{1}/_{2}$ to 3 cups, maybe more depending on the size of the dish). Cover with aluminum foil. Put the lamb and the fennel in the oven and cook until the fennel is very soft and the lamb is medium-rare (135°F.), about 1 hour for the fennel, and about $1^{1}/_{2}$ hours for the lamb. Let the lamb rest for 10 minutes before slicing.

When the lamb is ready to slice, make the walnuts. Melt the butter in a skillet over medium heat. Add the walnuts and cook, stirring, until toasted and browned, 3 to 4 minutes. Stir in the sugar, parsley, and chile, season with salt and pepper, and cook just to wilt the chile, 1 to 2 more minutes. Slice the lamb against the grain and serve it with the fennel, Romesco sauce, and walnuts.

NOTE | Ask your butcher to remove the longer thighbone (from the fatter part of the leg) but leave the shorter shank bone (from the narrow end of the leg), so that the leg will hold its shape. With the thigh bone removed, you'll be able to open out that part of the leg, like a book, and coat it with the herb mixture to flavor the inside of the meat as it cooks.

5 garlic cloves, minced

$^{1}/_{2}$ bunch of fresh flat-leaf parsley, chopped

1 tablespoon extra-virgin olive oil

Kosher salt and freshly ground black pepper

1 leg of lamb (about 7 pounds), thighbone removed (see Note)

1 recipe Turkish Spice Mix (page 28)

FENNEL CONFIT

3 fennel bulbs, trimmed and quartered

Kosher salt and freshly ground black pepper

Juice of 1 lemon

Extra-virgin olive oil

SWEET WALNUTS

2 tablespoons unsalted butter

1 cup walnut pieces

2 tablespoons brown sugar

$^{1}/_{4}$ cup chopped fresh flat-leaf parsley

1 fresh hot red chile, seeded and thinly sliced crosswise

Kosher salt and freshly ground black pepper

1 recipe Romesco Sauce (page 19)

Greek Lamb Pie

1 hour + baking time | Serves 6 to 8

This is a hearty winter dish, a truly satisfying casserole. If you can't find a butcher who carries fresh lamb, ground beef works just as well.

3 large eggplants (about 2$\frac{1}{4}$ pounds total)

Kosher salt and freshly ground black pepper

Extra-virgin olive oil

1 medium onion, chopped

3 garlic cloves, minced

$\frac{1}{2}$ lemon, sliced into thin rounds

1 handful of fresh oregano, chopped

2 handfuls of fresh flat-leaf parsley, chopped

2 pounds ground lamb

1 cinnamon stick

3 tablespoons tomato paste

1 (14-ounce) can whole, peeled tomatoes, drained and hand crushed

8 ounces feta cheese, crumbled

1 $\frac{1}{4}$ cups freshly grated Parmigiano-Reggiano cheese

1 cup fresh bread crumbs (see Note)

First get the eggplant going. Cut off the stems, peel the eggplants with a vegetable peeler or a knife, and slice lengthwise $\frac{1}{2}$ inch thick. Season the slices on both sides with salt and pepper. Coat a large skillet with a 3-count of oil and put it over medium heat. When the oil is hot, add as many slices as will fit in a single layer in the pan and fry, turning once, until browned on both sides, 4 to 5 minutes per side. Do this in several batches, and add a little bit more oil if you need to. Remove the eggplant slices to a paper-towel–lined platter to drain.

Add a 2-count of oil to the pan and toss in the onion, garlic, lemon slices, oregano, and parsley. Cook, stirring, until soft and fragrant, about 3 minutes. Break the ground lamb into chunks and put that into the pan. Stir to break up the meat. Season with salt and pepper, and toss in the cinnamon stick. Stir in the tomato paste and hand-crushed tomatoes. Simmer for about 10 minutes, stirring occasionally, until all of the liquid has evaporated. Remove from the heat and pick out the cinnamon stick.

Preheat the oven to 350°F. Get your baking dish ready for the layering. Line the bottom of a 9 × 13-inch glass or ceramic baking dish with one third of the eggplant slices. They should completely cover the bottom, with no gaps. Spread half of the lamb sauce over the eggplant, smoothing it with a spatula. Sprinkle with half of the feta and $\frac{1}{2}$ cup of the Parmigiano cheese. Repeat the layering again, ending with a final layer of eggplant. Toss the bread crumbs with the remaining $\frac{1}{4}$ cup of Parmigiano cheese, a 2-count of olive oil, and salt; sprinkle the mixture over the top in a nice even layer. Cover with aluminum foil and bake for 20 minutes. Then uncover and bake until the top is golden, 10 to 20 more minutes. Let cool for 10 minutes before serving. Watch your guests just tear through this!

NOTE | For 1 cup of bread crumbs, cut the crusts off of 3 slices of bread and pulse in a food processor.

THE WORLDWIDE BUTCHER TOUR.
SPONSORED BY NIKE.

Lamb Shanks Braised in Red Wine and Cinnamon

2¼ hours + 4 to 6 hours marinating time | **Serves 4**

This dish is inspired by the flavors of a Moroccan lamb tagine but it's no more difficult to make than a pot roast. The rich lamb falls off the bone and melts in your mouth and the olives and apricots give it a salty-sweet finish. This is truly a great dish.

4 lamb shanks (about 8 ounces each)

Kosher salt and freshly ground black pepper

6 fresh thyme sprigs

2 fresh rosemary sprigs

Zest of 1 lemon, peeled in big strips

2 garlic cloves, halved

½ teaspoon whole cloves

2 cinnamon sticks

1 teaspoon whole black peppercorns

2 bay leaves

1 tablespoon sugar

1 bottle full-bodied red wine, such as Cabernet Sauvignon

¼ cup all-purpose flour

3 tablespoons extra-virgin olive oil

2 cups lamb stock or chicken stock, homemade (see page 36) or store-bought

1 cup pearl onions, peeled

3 carrots, peeled and coarsely chopped

12 large green Spanish olives

12 dried apricots

First off, you want to marinate the lamb shanks for a few hours to permeate the meat with deep flavor. The wine also tenderizes the meat. Put the shanks in a large glass bowl and season with salt and pepper. Break up the thyme and rosemary with your hands to release the oils and toss them on top of the lamb. Add the lemon zest, garlic, cloves, cinnamon, peppercorns, bay leaves, and sugar. Pour in the wine, cover, and refrigerate for 4 to 6 hours.

When you're ready to cook, pull the lamb shanks out of the marinade (reserve it), and lay them out on some paper towels. Pat the meat dry with more paper towels. Put the flour in a large shallow platter and season it with a fair amount of salt and pepper. Dredge the lamb shanks in the seasoned flour and pat off the excess.

Put a large Dutch oven or other heavy-bottomed pot over medium-high heat and add the oil. When the oil is almost smoking, add the lamb shanks and cook, turning carefully with tongs, until they are a caramel-brown color all over. This will take 7 to 10 minutes. Drizzle with a little more oil if needed. (Cook the shanks in batches if the pan is crowded.) Add the reserved marinade to the pot, bring to a simmer, and cook until slightly reduced, about 5 minutes. Now pour in the stock and add the onions, carrots, olives, and apricots. Bring to a boil, cover the pot, drop the heat to low, and simmer until the lamb is tender and the meat is falling off the bone, 1½ to 2 hours.

Transfer the lamb shanks to a large platter and spoon the onions, carrots, olives, and apricots over them. Strain the braising juices and season with salt and pepper. Pour the sauce over everything and serve immediately with some really good, crusty bread.

Potted Rabbit with Baby Pears and Creamy Polenta

2 hours | Serves 4

I was working on the *Ultimate* with a friend of mine, Rosemary Schraeger, a great cook who has a show on the BBC. We hung out together for an afternoon in a castle in Devon in the south of England, and she made a dish similar to this but using baby chicken. I wanted to make it when I got back to New York, but I couldn't find baby chicken. The rabbit looked good so I used that instead.

Most of the meat on a rabbit is in the legs and saddle. Ask your butcher to cut it into six pieces: the saddle split in half crosswise, and each leg split in two at the joint. (You can throw the forelegs into the pot too, but there's not much meat on them.)

Wrap each rabbit piece in pancetta and secure it with a toothpick. Combine the red wine, vegetables, garlic, herbs, and sugar in a large bowl. Add the rabbit pieces. Cover and marinate in the refrigerator for at least 4 hours, or overnight.

Remove the rabbit from the marinade and pat the pieces dry. Spoon out the vegetables and discard. (Leave the herbs in the bowl with the wine.) Put the flour in a large, shallow platter and season with a fair amount of salt and pepper. (Taste it; it should taste well seasoned.) Heat a 3-count of oil in a large enameled pot or Dutch oven over medium heat. Dredge the rabbit pieces in the flour and pat off the excess. Sear the rabbit pieces, turning with tongs, until they are a rich brown color all over. (Don't crowd the pot or the rabbit won't brown easily; cook in batches if you need to.)

Take the rabbit out of the pot with the tongs and put it on a plate. Now pour in the wine with the herbs and stir to scrape up all of the browned bits on the bottom of the pot. Pour in 2 cups of the chicken stock, then return the rabbit pieces to the pot. Add more stock if necessary to cover the rabbit entirely. Bring the whole thing up to a simmer, cover, and simmer very slowly on top of the stove until the rabbit is tender, 1 to 1¼ hours.

While the rabbit is cooking, preheat the oven to 425°F. Coat a roasting pan with olive oil. Season the pears with salt and pepper and place them, cut sides down, in the pan. Put the pan over medium-high heat and cook until the cut sides are browned. Now scatter the chestnuts

{ *recipe continues* }

RABBIT

1 rabbit (about 3 pounds), cut into 6 pieces

6 slices pancetta or bacon

1 bottle dry red wine

1 carrot, peeled and chopped

1 onion, chopped

1 leek, chopped, white part only

3 garlic cloves, whacked with the side of a large knife

2 fresh rosemary sprigs

½ bunch of fresh sage

Pinch of sugar

1 cup all-purpose flour

Kosher salt and freshly ground black pepper

Extra-virgin olive oil

2 to 3 cups chicken stock, homemade (see page 36) or store-bought

TO SERVE

Extra-virgin olive oil

6 baby or other small pears, such as
    seckle, cut in half (do not peel or
    core)

Kosher salt and freshly ground
    black pepper

1 (7.4-ounce) can cooked chestnuts,
    drained

Leaves from 1 sprig of fresh sage

Creamy Polenta with Parmigiano and
    Butter (recipe follows)

1 handful of arugula

Juice of $\frac{1}{2}$ lemon

over the top, throw the sage on top of that, drizzle with a little more oil, and roast until the pears and chestnuts are cooked through, 20 to 25 more minutes.

When the rabbit is cooked, taste the sauce for seasoning. Remove the toothpicks. Serve the rabbit with the sauce, the pears and chestnuts, and creamy polenta. Toss the arugula with a drizzle of olive oil, the lemon juice, and salt and pepper. Serve alongside as garnish.

Creamy Polenta with Parmigiano and Butter   30 minutes | Serves 8

2 cups chicken stock, homemade (see page 36) or store-bought | $\frac{1}{2}$ cup heavy cream | $\frac{3}{4}$ cup polenta or yellow cornmeal | $\frac{1}{3}$ cup freshly grated Parmigiano-Reggiano cheese | $\frac{1}{4}$ cup ($\frac{1}{2}$ stick) unsalted butter, at room temperature | Kosher salt and freshly ground black pepper

In a saucepan over medium-low heat, bring the stock and cream to a simmer. Slowly whisk in the polenta and reduce the heat to low. Continue to cook for about 20 minutes, stirring often to prevent lumps. The polenta should absorb most of the liquid but still be creamy.

Remove the pan from the heat and stir in the cheese, butter, salt, and pepper. Taste and adjust seasonings. Serve immediately.

Chicken Parmesan (the Classic)

1 hour | Serves 4

Coat a sauté pan with a 2-count of olive oil and put it over medium heat. When the oil gets hazy, add the onion, garlic, and bay leaves and cook, stirring, for 5 minutes to soften. Add the olives and about half of the torn basil leaves. Carefully add the tomatoes (nothing splashes like tomatoes), sugar, and salt and pepper and cook, stirring every now and then, until the liquid is cooked down and the sauce is thick, about 15 minutes. Taste for salt and pepper. Lower the heat, cover, and keep warm.

Preheat the oven to 450°F. Bring a large pot of lightly salted water to a boil for the spaghetti.

Now get yourself set up to cook the chicken. Put the flour in a shallow platter, season with a fair amount of salt and pepper, and mix with your fingers so that the seasoning is incorporated. Taste: The flour should be quite well seasoned. In a wide bowl, beat the eggs and water until frothy. Put the bread crumbs on a plate, season with the chopped parsley, chopped basil, and salt and pepper.

Put the chicken breasts side by side on a cutting board and lay a piece of plastic wrap over them. Pound the chicken breasts to about $1/2$ inch thick with a flat meat mallet, the bottom of a heavy saucepan, or the side of a bottle.

Coat a large ovenproof skillet with a 3-count of olive oil and put it over medium-high heat. Lightly dredge the chicken cutlets in the seasoned flour and pat off the excess. Dip them in the beaten egg to coat completely and let the excess drip off. Then dredge the breasts in the bread crumbs. When the oil is nice and hot, add the cutlets and fry for 2 minutes on each side, or until golden and crispy.

Pour the tomato–olive sauce over the chicken in the pan and sprinkle with the mozzarella and Parmigiano cheeses. Drizzle with olive oil, and then toss in the rest of the torn basil. Put the skillet in the oven and bake the chicken for about 15 minutes, until the cheese is bubbly. When the chicken has about 10 minutes to go, drop the spaghetti into the boiling water and cook until al dente, 8 to 10 minutes. Drain, and serve with the chicken.

Extra-virgin olive oil

1 medium onion, diced

2 garlic cloves, minced

2 bay leaves

$1/2$ cup kalamata olives, pitted

$1/2$ bunch of fresh basil leaves, torn into pieces, plus 1 tablespoon chopped fresh basil

2 (28-ounce) cans whole, peeled tomatoes, drained and hand crushed

Pinch of sugar

Kosher salt and freshly ground black pepper

$3/4$ cup all-purpose flour

2 large eggs, lightly beaten with about 1 tablespoon water

1 cup dried bread crumbs

1 tablespoon fresh flat-leaf parsley, chopped

4 skinless, boneless chicken breasts (about 1 $1/2$ pounds total)

1 (8-ounce) ball of fresh mozzarella di bufala, drained and shredded

Freshly grated Parmigiano-Reggiano cheese

1 pound dried, good-quality spaghetti

COME ON, THIS WON'T HURT A BIT.
YOU AND I HAVE A DATE WITH A WOK.

Stir-Fried Dungeness Crab with Sweet Chili Sauce and Bok Choy

1 hour | Serves 4

You'll need crab crackers, mini forks, a side bowl for the shells, a stack of napkins, and bowls of warm lemon water to clean your hands. Serve this with steamed white rice.

First thing to do is "dismantle" the crabs. Bring a big pot of salted water to a boil, toss in the live crabs, and boil for 2 minutes. Drain the crabs and let them cool. When the crabs are cool enough to handle, place them top side up on your work surface. Stick your thumb under the edge of the top shells, pull forward, and lift the shells up and off; set those aside, you'll need them later. Now scrape out the gills that you'll find under the shells. Turn the crabs over. On the underbellies, you'll find a triangular flap called the "apron." Pull these off, too. Finally, rinse the crabs of all the gray or green spongy stuff (the soft yellow matter is fat, or crab butter, and considered desirable by many; keep it if you like). Cut the crabs into quarters with a big knife, leaving the legs attached.

Heat the peanut oil in a wok over high heat until almost smoking. Add the garlic, ginger, chiles, and bok choy and stir-fry for 1 minute. Remove to a side platter. Toss in the crab pieces, including the reserved top shells. Cook, stirring, for about a minute, then take out the top shells and stir-fry for 3 more minutes. With a big spoon or spatula, remove the crab pieces to the side platter.

Now you're going to make a sauce in the wok. Pour in 1 cup of water. Add the brown sugar, soy sauce, lemon juice, and sake. Stir that around for about 2 minutes to dissolve the sugar. Give the cornstarch slurry a stir, stir that in, too, and cook for another minute, or until the sauce thickens. Return the crabs and bok choy to the pan, toss everything together to coat, cover the wok, and cook for 3 minutes.

To serve, line a large platter with butter lettuce leaves, and arrange the crabs with the top shells back on top so they look roughly like whole crabs again—cool, right? Put the bok choy around the crab and pour the sauce over the whole thing. Garnish with the green onions and peanuts.

2 live Dungeness crabs,
  1 $^1/_2$ pounds each
$^1/_4$ cup peanut oil
3 garlic cloves, chopped
1-inch piece of fresh ginger, peeled
  and grated
2 fresh red chiles, sliced
4 heads of baby bok choy, halved
$^1/_4$ cup dark brown sugar
$^1/_4$ cup low-sodium soy sauce
Juice of $^1/_2$ lemon
$^1/_4$ cup sake
1 tablespoon cornstarch mixed
  with 2 tablespoons water, to
  make a slurry
Butter lettuce leaves, for serving
2 chopped green onions, white and
  green parts, for garnish
$^1/_4$ cup chopped unsalted peanuts,
  for garnish

Pan-Seared Scallops with Soft Wheat and Porcinis

1 hour | Serves 4

I came up with this recipe for the City Harvest event last year in New York City. City Harvest is a nonprofit organization that collects food from the best restaurants in the city to feed homeless people. It was a huge hit.

I can't tell you how crazy I am about fresh porcinis. They start hitting the marketplace around late September and last through early December. The porcinis and the wheat are cooked risotto style and the wheat absorbs all the meaty flavor from the porcinis. With the pomegranate seeds, the buttery scallops, the mushrooms, and the wheat, this is a great fall bite; when you close your eyes you know exactly where you stand inside the calendar.

Extra-virgin olive oil

3 shallots, minced

2 garlic cloves, minced

¹/₂ pound fresh porcini or cremini mushrooms (or whatever mushrooms you find in your supermarket), wiped clean and sliced

Kosher salt and freshly ground black pepper

2 cups farro (spelt)

2 teaspoons fresh thyme leaves

¹/₂ cup white wine

2 cups chicken stock, homemade (see page 36) or store-bought

¹/₄ cup heavy cream

2 tablespoons unsalted butter

Juice of ¹/₂ lemon

1 pound large sea scallops

1 recipe Pomegranate, Walnut, Celery Leaf, and Parsley Sauce (page 24)

1 bunch of purslane (optional)

Heat a 2-count of oil in a large sauté pan over medium heat. Add the shallots and garlic and cook for 3 minutes, or until the shallots are translucent. Toss in the mushrooms and cook down until they have lost their moisture and are golden brown, about 10 minutes. Season with salt and pepper. Add the farro and thyme and stir until the grains are coated with the oil mixture. Add the white wine and boil to evaporate the alcohol. Now begin adding the chicken stock, one ladle at a time, and simmering until the grains have absorbed the liquid before adding the next ladle. Stir constantly. You want to cook the farro until it is still slightly firm—not at all mushy—10 to 12 minutes. (You may not need to use all of the stock.) When the farro has reached the right consistency, stir in the heavy cream, butter, and lemon juice, and season with salt and pepper. Reduce the heat to low to keep the farro warm while you cook the scallops.

Season the scallops with salt and pepper. Put a large sauté pan over medium-high heat and drizzle in a 2-count of oil. When the oil is almost smoking, add the scallops and sear for 30 seconds on each side.

To serve, divide the farro among 4 plates. Top with seared scallops and sprinkle with the pomegranate sauce. Garnish with purslane, if you're using it.

Rolled, Roasted Salmon Stuffed with Creamed Leeks

1 ¼ hours | Serves 6

I wrote this recipe after going fishing for wild Pacific salmon off the Oregon coast with my friend, Greg Higgins, the chef at Higgins restaurant in Portland. Greg is a true champion of organic, sustainable agriculture on the west coast. After hanging out with him for a couple of days I really understood the importance of supporting the wild salmon industry. Wild salmon tastes like the ocean, and in my opinion, its flavor is far superior to that of farmed. Pacific wild salmon is available from the spring into the fall.

Extra-virgin olive oil

2 leeks, white and light green parts only, cut into paper-thin rounds

2 garlic cloves, minced

Leaves from ¹/₂ bunch of fresh thyme

¹/₂ cup heavy cream

Juice of ¹/₂ lemon

Kosher salt and freshly ground black pepper

MUSHROOM GRAVY

Extra-virgin olive oil

3 pounds assorted mushrooms, wiped clean, stemmed or trimmed, and sliced

3 garlic cloves, minced

Leaves from ¹/₂ bunch of fresh thyme

¹/₂ cup dry white wine

Kosher salt and freshly ground black pepper

3 cups Roasted Veal Stock with Red Wine (page 38)

1 whole salmon fillet (about 3 pounds, preferably wild), with skin, scaled and pin bones removed

In a large skillet, heat a 2-count of olive oil over medium heat. Add the leeks, garlic, and thyme and cook until the leeks are softened but not colored, 3 to 5 minutes. Add the cream and simmer until almost dry. Season with the lemon juice and salt and pepper. Spread the leek mixture out on a plate and put it in the freezer to cool quickly (not to freeze).

At this point, turn your attention to the mushrooms: You're going to make a thick mushroom gravy. Get yourself a big sauté pan and coat it with ¼ cup of olive oil. Put it over medium-high heat and get the oil smoking hot. Add the mushrooms, garlic, and thyme and sauté for 10 to 15 minutes to get some color on the mushrooms. Add the wine and simmer that until the pan is dry. Season with salt and pepper and add the veal stock. Bring to a boil, reduce the heat, and simmer very slowly to reduce the stock over the mushrooms until it thickens to a sauce consistency, 15 to 20 minutes.

While that's going, you can prepare the salmon. Preheat the oven to 450°F. Put a baking sheet in the oven and get it good and hot.

Put the salmon fillet, skin side down, on a cutting board so the tail points toward you. Using a sharp knife and working from the right side of the fillet toward the left, split the salmon fillet almost in half width-wise, but do not slice completely through the opposite (left) side. Now turn the salmon 90 degrees to lay it crosswise on the cutting board, so that the cut edge of the fillet is away from you. Lift the top half of the fillet up and over, like opening a book. Season the inside with salt and pepper. Spread the cooled leek mixture evenly over both "pages" of the open fish. Then beginning with the bottom "page" (the edge closest to you), begin rolling the salmon fillet up and over itself, like a jelly roll. The salmon should roll up so that the skin covers the outside of the fish again. Cut several lengths of kitchen twine and tie the salmon roll in several places. Sprinkle the outside of the roast with salt and pepper.

Open the oven and drizzle a 2-count of olive oil over the baking sheet to coat it. Close the oven and let the oil heat until it's smoking. Then, using heavy oven mitts or a couple of thick towels folded into a square, remove the hot baking sheet from the oven and put it on the stovetop. Put the salmon roast on the baking sheet, skin side down. Pop that back in the oven and roast it until the salmon is just cooked through, about 15 minutes. Carefully take the pan out of the oven and let the salmon rest for 5 to 10 minutes.

To serve, cut the salmon into slices and serve with a spoonful of the mushroom gravy.

Honey- and Soy-Roasted Squab with Curried Green Apples

1 hour | Serves 4

The first time I tasted squab, ten or fifteen years ago, I was astounded at how amazing it tasted. Then I moved to Chinatown in New York City and the restaurant on the corner had squab on the menu. So I got inspired to cook squab with soy and honey, flavors reminiscent of Chinatown. The salty-sweet flavor of the glaze deeply complements the rich taste of the bird.

Put two large cast-iron (or regular ovenproof) skillets over medium heat. Divide the butter and honey between the pans. Season the birds on both sides with a fair amount of salt and pepper and put them in the pans, skin sides down. Cook for 5 to 7 minutes, or until the skin gets crispy. (If the honey starts to burn, turn the heat down.) Flatten the birds with a spatula while they're cooking to keep the skins in contact with the pans. Flip the birds, brush the skins with the soy sauce, and continue cooking for about 15 minutes, or until the squab are cooked to medium-rare. Drizzle with the pan juices and serve hot accompanied by the Parsley, Green Apple, and Curry Sauce.

8 tablespoons (1 stick) unsalted butter

$^1\!/_4$ cup honey

4 squab, backbones removed, breastbones cracked, and birds flattened

Kosher salt and freshly ground black pepper

$^1\!/_4$ cup low-sodium soy sauce

1 recipe Parsley, Green Apple, and Curry Sauce (page 22)

Salt-Crusted Potatoes **1$^1\!/_2$ hours | Serves 4**

This is my favorite new way to cook the spud: in a huge casserole full of kosher salt and fresh herbs with new potatoes buried in the salt. Absolutely delicious.

2 cups kosher salt | Several turns of coarsely ground black pepper | Needles from 2 sprigs of fresh rosemary | Leaves from 4 sprigs of fresh thyme | 12 small yellow potatoes, such as fingerling or Yukon Gold | $^1\!/_2$ cup extra-virgin olive oil

Combine the salt, pepper, and herbs in a large bowl and mix it all up with your fingers. Set aside. Rinse, scrub, and pat dry the potatoes.

Pour the oil into a large cast-iron skillet and set it over medium-high heat. When the oil reaches a slight smoke, add the potatoes in a single layer and fry until the skins get nice and crackled on all sides. Lower the heat to medium, cover the potatoes completely with the salt mixture, and cook for about 1$^1\!/_2$ hours, or until the salt forms a crust; the potatoes will be tender. Pull the potatoes out of the salt crust and serve hot.

Maple-Roasted Turkey with Cornbread Stuffing

1 hour + about 3 hours roasting time | Serves 12

Some guy walked up to me on the street about three weeks ago. He said that he had downloaded my roast turkey recipe from the Internet and that it had saved Thanksgiving for him. I really appreciated hearing that. Roasted turkey at Thanksgiving sends me to the floor. This is a straightforward approach to roasting the whole bird. Serve it with Whipped Sweet Potatoes and Bananas with Honey (page 234).

1 cup (2 sticks) unsalted butter, softened to room temperature

1/2 bunch of fresh sage, finely chopped

Kosher salt and freshly ground black pepper

2 large onions, finely chopped

12 large cornbread muffins, torn into pieces, or 1 loaf of cornbread, cubed (about 6 cups)

1 egg, lightly beaten

1/2 cup heavy cream

3 cups chicken stock, homemade (see page 36) or store-bought

1 (12- to 14-pound) fresh turkey, giblets, neck, and liver discarded

1/2 cup maple syrup

2 tablespoons hot water

8 strips bacon

1/4 cup all-purpose flour

Juice of 1/2 lemon

Preheat the oven to 350°F. and remove the top rack of the oven.

Put the butter and sage in a mixing bowl and mash with a fork or spoon until the sage is well incorporated. Season with salt and pepper. Put about half of that in a sauté pan and melt over medium heat. (Reserve the rest for the turkey.) Add the onions and cook for 10 minutes, or until soft and golden. Scrape all that into a large mixing bowl, add the cornbread pieces, season well with salt and pepper, and give it a good toss until it's well combined. In a separate bowl, whisk together the egg, cream, and 1/2 cup of the stock, and pour that over the cornbread. Stir the stuffing together and set it aside while you work on the turkey.

Rinse the bird thoroughly inside and out with cold water, and pat dry with paper towels. Sprinkle the cavity and skin liberally with salt and pepper. Using your fingers, gently lift the skin from the turkey breast and slip the remaining seasoned butter under, massaging the breast meat as you go. Stuff the bird with the cornbread stuffing and truss it (or just cross the legs over one another and tie with a piece of kitchen twine). Put the turkey on a rack in a large roasting pan, and into the oven.

In a small bowl, stir the maple syrup with the hot water to thin. Roast the turkey for 2 hours, basting with the maple glaze every 30 minutes. Then pull the oven rack out a bit so you can get at the turkey and shingle the bacon over the breast so it's totally covered. Continue cooking until an instant-read thermometer inserted into the meaty part of the thigh registers 170°F. The thigh juices will run clear when pricked with a knife, about 3 hours total (15 minutes per pound). If the legs or breast brown too quickly during roasting, cover them with foil. Take the turkey out of the oven and put the roasting pan on the stovetop. Transfer the turkey to a serving tray to rest while you make the gravy.

[recipe continues]

Skim off most of the fat from the pan drippings with a spoon and put the roasting pan across two burners, over medium-high heat. Using a wooden spoon, scrape up the browned bits stuck to the bottom of the pan. Whisk in the flour, stirring as it thickens to prevent lumps. Pour in the remaining $2\frac{1}{2}$ cups of stock, $\frac{1}{2}$ cup at a time, stirring constantly to blend and prevent lumps. Bring to a simmer; season with salt and pepper and a squeeze of lemon juice to brighten the flavors. Simmer for 5 minutes and then strain to remove the bits. Carve the turkey and serve with the gravy and stuffing.

Whipped Sweet Potatoes and Bananas with Honey 30 minutes + roasting time | Serves 12

This is a very personal recipe I've been making for years. It has kind of turned into The Thing I make at Thanksgiving and people love it. The bananas give it such a good flavor. If you like, you can roast the potatoes and bananas ahead of time, then put it all together just before serving. Count on an extra 10 minutes or so to heat it in the oven.

10 medium-size sweet potatoes, scrubbed | 4 bananas, unpeeled | 1 cup (2 sticks) unsalted butter, at room temperature | $\frac{1}{3}$ cup honey | Kosher salt | $\frac{3}{4}$ cup dark brown sugar | $\frac{1}{2}$ cup all-purpose flour | $1\frac{1}{2}$ cups pecans, chopped

Preheat the oven to 400°F. Prick the sweet potatoes all over with a fork, put them in a roasting pan, and roast for 30 minutes. Toss the bananas into the pan and continue roasting for 10 to 15 minutes, until both the bananas and potatoes are very soft. Remove the pan from the oven but don't turn the oven off.

When the potatoes are cool enough to handle, scoop out the flesh into a large mixing bowl. Peel the bananas and add them to the bowl along with 1 stick of the butter and the honey. Season with salt and beat vigorously with a wooden spoon until everything's well combined and the mixture is fluffy. Spoon that into an ovenproof serving bowl and smooth the top.

In a separate mixing bowl, use your fingers to rub together the remaining stick of butter, the brown sugar, flour, and pecans until the mixture is the consistency of coarse crumbs. Sprinkle the crumb mixture over the sweet potatoes and return to the oven. Bake for 20 minutes, or until the crumbs are golden. Serve hot.

APPLES

IN MY OPINION, APPLES ARE THE UNDISPUTED HEAVYWEIGHT CHAMPS OF THE FALL SEASON. I KEEP A BOWL OF FARMSTAND APPLES IN MY KITCHEN AND USE THEM IN EVERYTHING; SLICED PAPER-THIN TO SERVE WITH RAW TUNA, IN DESSERTS, AND SLOW COOKED IN SAVORY RECIPES LIKE THE DUCK ON THE FOLLOWING PAGE.

Crisp Roasted Duck with Apples and Prunes and Roasted Onions

3 to 3$^{1}/_{2}$ hours + 24 hours in the fridge | **Serves 4**

Mmmm. I made up this dish when I had family in town for the weekend and I wanted to make a real showstopper. I learned in Chinatown that the way to get crisp skin on a duck is to dry it for a day in the refrigerator, uncovered, in front of the fan. Serve with Buttery Turnips (page 240).

Rinse the duck thoroughly, inside and out, and pat dry with paper towels. Then stick it in the refrigerator on a clean tea towel right in front of the fan, and let the fan blow on it for 24 hours. When you're ready to cook, trim off as much fat as possible from all over the duck. Then season the bird inside and out with a generous amount of salt and pepper. Do not prick the skin—that makes the skin chewy and soggy.

Now make the stuffing. Melt the butter in a large skillet over medium heat. Add the onion, celery, celery seed, prunes, apples, and 4 sage leaves. Season with salt and pepper and sauté for about 10 minutes, until the vegetables are soft. Add the bread cubes and stir together. Dump the stuffing out into a large mixing bowl and moisten with a squeeze of lemon and the heavy cream. Give it another good toss and season well with salt and pepper. Spoon the stuffing into the duck cavity. Fold the wing tips back behind the wings.

Preheat the oven to 375°F. Get yourself a roasting pan with a rack large enough to hold the duck. Tear off a foot-long piece of aluminum foil and lay it on the rack, letting a bit of the foil hang off one end. Lay the duck, breast side up, on the foil so the stuffed end of the duck is at the end with the extra foil. Fold that extra foil over the stuffing; the foil will protect the stuffing from burning and falling into the yummy duck fat. Roast the duck for 2$^{1}/_{2}$ to 3 hours, until an instant-read thermometer inserted into the thigh measures 180°F. and the legs wiggle easily. Rotate the pan every 20 minutes or so; it may seem like a bother, but it's the best way to ensure an even, crispy skin. When the duck is done, pull it out of the oven, leaving the oven on. Lift the rack out of the pan and set the duck on a cutting board to let it rest before carving. Now you have a whole lot of duck fat in the bottom of the roasting pan. You're going to use it to make fantastic roasted onions. So pour $^{1}/_{2}$ cup of the fat into a large oven-proof skillet. Reserve a couple of tablespoons of fat in the roasting pan—you'll use it to make the gravy, so set it aside for a moment. Pour any remaining fat into a container and save it for something else.

{ recipe continues }

---

1 duckling (about 5 pounds)

Kosher salt and freshly ground
   black pepper

2 tablespoons unsalted butter

1 onion, chopped

2 celery stalks, chopped

$^{1}/_{2}$ teaspoon celery seed

1 cup pitted prunes, halved

3 Golden Delicious apples, peeled,
   cored, and cut into wedges

8 fresh sage leaves

$^{1}/_{4}$ loaf of rye bread, crusts removed,
   cubed, and dried overnight
   (about 2 cups)

Juice of $^{1}/_{2}$ lemon

$^{1}/_{2}$ cup heavy cream

ROASTED ONIONS

1 pound cipolline onions, peeled

5 sprigs of fresh thyme

Kosher salt and freshly ground
   black pepper

2 tablespoons all-purpose flour

1 cup fruity red wine, such as
   Pinot Noir

2 cups chicken stock, homemade
   (see page 36) or store-bought

Back to the onions now. Put the skillet over medium heat. When the fat is nice and hot, add the onions and toss to coat them in the fat. Cook for 5 minutes, or until the onions begin to caramelize. Add the thyme, and season with salt and pepper. Stick the pan in the oven and roast for 15 minutes, or until the onions are soft and slightly charred.

Meanwhile, make the gravy. Set the roasting pan across two burners, over medium heat. Sprinkle in the flour and stir to make a paste. Crank the heat up to high and add the wine. Cook, stirring and scraping the bottom of the pan to get up all the brown bits, until the liquid has reduced slightly. Add the chicken stock and the remaining 4 sage leaves, season with salt and pepper, and cook, stirring, for a minute or two, until the gravy has thickened slightly. Carve the duck and serve with the stuffing, gravy, and roasted onions.

Buttery Turnips 1 hour | Serves 6

I wrote this for *Bon Appétit* last Christmas. The turnips are really rich, boiled and mashed like mashed potatoes, with cream and butter. The anchovy-walnut topping is kind of a Turkish thing—rich and salty on top of the purée. It's delicious.

3 pounds turnips, peeled and cut into pieces | 2 garlic cloves, peeled but left whole | Kosher salt and freshly ground black pepper | 2 tablespoons extra-virgin olive oil | 3 anchovy fillets | $^1/_2$ cup walnuts, chopped | 4 tablespoons ($^1/_2$ stick) unsalted butter | 1 cup heavy cream | $^1/_4$ bunch of fresh flat-leaf parsley, finely chopped | Juice of $^1/_2$ lemon

Put the turnips and garlic in a large pot and add cold water to cover. Season generously with salt. Bring the water to a boil, reduce the heat, and simmer for about 30 minutes, or until the turnips are fork tender. Drain in a colander and pass the turnips and garlic through a ricer or food mill into a large serving bowl. Set that aside.

Heat a 2-count of olive oil in a sauté pan over medium-low heat. Toss in the anchovy fillets and cook, crushing them with a wooden spoon until they dissolve into the oil. Add the walnuts and stir to combine. Cook for 3 to 5 minutes, stirring. Take the pan off the heat.

Meanwhile, warm the butter and cream in a small saucepan over medium heat until hot but not boiling. Season with salt and pepper and fold into the riced turnips. Taste for seasoning. Stir the parsley and lemon juice into the walnut mixture, and scatter that all over the turnips. Serve hot.

Veal Saltimbocca Alla Romana

45 minutes | Serves 4

This is a dish made famous in the small trattorias of Rome. It's classic, impressive, and incredibly easy. And the side dishes—Baked Polenta with Brown Butter and Pine Nuts (page 244) and Braised Escarole with Garlic and Lemon (page 245)—work really well with it.

Put the veal cutlets side by side on a sheet of plastic wrap or wax paper. Lay a piece of prosciutto on top of each cutlet and cover with another piece of plastic or wax paper. Gently flatten the cutlets with a rolling pin or meat mallet, until the pieces are about ¼ inch thick and the prosciutto has adhered to the veal. Remove the plastic or wax paper and lay a couple of sage leaves in the center of each cutlet. Weave a toothpick in and out of the veal to secure the prosciutto and sage.

Put the flour in a shallow platter and season with a fair amount of salt and pepper. Mix with your fingers to incorporate the seasoning. Taste the flour; it should be well seasoned. Now dredge the veal in the seasoned flour and pat off the excess.

Heat the oil and 1 tablespoon of the butter in a large skillet over medium heat. When the butter stops foaming, put the veal in the pan, prosciutto side down, and cook for 3 minutes, or until crisp. Then flip the veal over and sauté the other side for 2 minutes, or until golden. Transfer the saltimbocca to a serving platter, remove the toothpicks, and keep warm while you make a quick pan sauce.

Add the wine to the pan, stirring to pick up all the delicious flavor stuck to the bottom. Let the wine cook down for a minute to burn off some of the alcohol. Add the chicken stock and the remaining tablespoon of butter, and swirl the pan around to emulsify. Season with salt and pepper. Pour the sauce over the saltimbocca, garnish with sage leaves and lemon wedges, and serve it while it's hot.

4 (5-ounce) thin-sliced veal cutlets

4 thin slices prosciutto

8 fresh sage leaves, plus more for garnish

¾ cup all-purpose flour, for dredging

Kosher salt and freshly ground black pepper

2 tablespoons extra-virgin olive oil

2 tablespoons unsalted butter

2 tablespoons dry white wine

¼ cup chicken stock, homemade (see page 36) or store-bought

Lemon wedges, for serving

Baked Polenta with Brown Butter and Pine Nuts   30 minutes | Serves 4

1 quart chicken stock, homemade (see page 36) or store-bought |
1 teaspoon kosher salt | **1 cup polenta or yellow cornmeal** | **$^1/_3$ cup heavy
cream** | **4 tablespoons ($^1/_2$ stick) unsalted butter** | **Kosher salt and freshly
ground black pepper** | **$^1/_4$ cup raisins** | **$^1/_4$ cup pine nuts** | **$^1/_2$ cup freshly
grated Parmigiano-Reggiano cheese**

Preheat the oven to 350°F. Butter a medium baking dish or gratin mold.
In a large pot, bring the chicken stock and salt to a boil over medium
heat. Gradually whisk in the polenta in a slow, steady stream. The liquid
will be absorbed and the polenta will lock up; don't freak, just whisk
through it. Lower the heat and continue to whisk until the polenta is
thick and smooth, about 20 minutes.

Add the cream and 2 tablespoons of the butter. Continue whisking
until it is incorporated and the polenta is creamy, about 5 minutes. Season
with salt and pepper. Pour into the buttered baking dish and bake until
firm, about 30 minutes.

To finish, put a small skillet over medium heat and add the remaining
2 tablespoons of butter. Swirl the pan over the heat and cook the butter
until golden and nutty, about 1 minute. Add the raisins and pine nuts,
tossing to coat in the brown butter. Put the polenta on a serving plate
and pour the raisins and pine nuts over the top. Sprinkle with the
Parmigiano cheese and serve.

Braised Escarole with Garlic and Lemon

30 minutes | Serves 4

1 head of escarole (about 1 pound) | ¼ cup extra-virgin olive oil | 1 tablespoon unsalted butter | 4 garlic cloves, sliced | ½ teaspoon dried red pepper flakes | 2 bay leaves | ½ lemon, cut in thin slices | Pinch of sugar | Kosher salt and freshly ground black pepper | 2 cups water or chicken stock, homemade (see page 36) or store-bought

Separate the escarole leaves and wash them individually, taking care to remove any soil at the base of the stems. Shake the leaves dry, stack them, and slice the escarole crosswise into ribbons about 1½ inches wide.

Place a large, deep skillet over medium heat and add the olive oil and butter. Toss in the garlic, red pepper flakes, bay leaves, and lemon slices. Cook, stirring for a couple of minutes, until you can smell everything cooking together. Nestle the escarole in the pan and sauté, stirring, until it begins to wilt and shrink down, about 2 minutes. Sprinkle with a pinch of sugar and season with salt and pepper. Pour in the water, cover, and simmer for 20 minutes, until the escarole is tender.

Roasted Pork Shoulder Stuffed with Caramelized Plantains

3¹/₂ hours + at least 3 hours to marinate the pork | Serves 8 to 10

A slow-roasted pork shoulder is one of the finest things I've ever eaten. I had a dish similar to this one years ago in the little surfer town of Rincon on the west coast of Puerto Rico. Roasted pork is well matched with a sweet flavor, like pork chops with applesauce. When it's cooked for 5 hours, the flavor as well as the texture of the pork gets moist and beautiful. And for a pork roast, shoulder is the only way to go. Serve with pigeon pea rice (recipe follows).

1 boneless pork shoulder (about
    4 pounds), skin on, if possible
    (see Note)

ADOBO

4 garlic cloves, smashed with the flat
    edge of a large knife
Leaves from ¹/₂ bunch of fresh
    oregano
4 tablespoons kosher salt (or
    1 tablespoon per pound of meat)
1 tablespoon coarsely ground
    black pepper
3 tablespoons vegetable oil
2 tablespoons white wine vinegar

FRIED SWEET PLANTAINS

4 ripe, black plantains
¹/₄ cup vegetable oil
Kosher salt

Place the pork, fat side up, on a cutting board. Using a sharp knife, score the surface of the meat with small slits. Then make a horizontal cut almost all the way through the middle of the roast so that it opens up like a book to make one big, flat piece of meat.

Now make an adobo to flavor the meat: Mash the garlic, oregano, salt, and pepper into a paste on a cutting board with the flat side of a knife. Scrape it into a bowl and stir in the oil and vinegar. Fold the roast up again and rub the adobo all over the outside of the pork, being sure to get into the incisions so the salt can penetrate the meat and pull out the moisture; this will help form a good, crisp crust on the outside of the roast. Cover the pork with plastic wrap, put it in the refrigerator, and marinate for at least 3 hours or up to overnight. When you're ready to cook, take the meat out of the refrigerator and let it sit at room temperature for 30 minutes before cooking.

Preheat the oven to 350°F. Peel the plantains and cut them in half crosswise on the bias, then slice in half lengthwise so you have 4 pieces each. Heat the oil in a large, heavy skillet over medium heat. Fry the plantains until golden on both sides, about 5 minutes per side. Remove to a plate lined with paper towels and sprinkle with salt.

Now open up the roast and lay the plantain halves on the bottom half. Fold the top half over the plantains and skewer the whole thing closed.

Put the pork into a roasting pan with a rack insert and roast for 3 hours, uncovered, until the skin is crispy and brown and the meat is very tender. Let the meat rest on a cutting board for 10 minutes before slicing.

NOTE | European cuts of pork often have skin. It's hard to find in the States but it makes for an amazing roast: The skin not only keeps the meat from drying, it also provides crispy and crackly snacking.

Puerto Rican–Style Pigeon Pea Rice

2 hours | Serves 6

This side dish is classic Puerto Rican food at its finest. Most of the food I discovered there is simple and rustic, but very delicious, almost like peasant food redefined.

1 pound dried pigeon peas, picked through and rinsed | 2 bay leaves | Kosher salt and freshly ground black pepper | $1/4$ cup canola oil | 1 medium onion, diced | 2 garlic cloves, minced | 1 green bell pepper, cored, seeded, and diced | 1 Cubanelle or Italian green pepper, cored, seeded, and diced | $1/2$ cup chicken stock, homemade (see page 36) or store-bought | $1/2$ teaspoon ground cumin | $1/2$ teaspoon ground coriander | $1/2$ teaspoon cayenne pepper | 2 cups long-grain rice | Juice of $1/2$ lime

Put the pigeon peas and bay leaves in a large pot. Cover with 3 quarts of cold water and put the pot over medium heat. Cover and cook until the peas are tender, about $1^{1}/_{2}$ hours. About halfway through the cooking, season with salt and pepper. This gives the beans time to soften so that the seasoning can penetrate. Check the water periodically and add more if necessary to keep the peas covered. Drain, reserving 4 cups of the cooking liquid.

Preheat the oven to 350°F. Coat a large Dutch oven or other oven-proof pot with the oil and put it over medium heat. When the oil begins to smoke, add the onion, garlic, and peppers and cook, stirring, for 10 minutes, or until the vegetables are softened but not browned. Pour in the chicken stock, bring to a simmer, and cook until the liquid has evaporated. Stir in the cumin, coriander, and cayenne. Stir in the rice and the cooked pigeon peas, along with the reserved 4 cups of cooking liquid. Add the lime juice and salt to taste and stir everything together. Cover and bake for 20 to 30 minutes, until the rice is tender and the liquid is absorbed.

Braised Pork Belly with Cider Gravy

1 ¹/₂ hours, including roasting time | **Serves 8**

Pork belly is nothing but a big slab of unsmoked bacon. But when you braise it slowly in apple cider, it becomes moist, delicious, and rustic, and cool à la Nigel Slater, who happens to be my favorite British cookbook writer.

Preheat the oven to 350°F. Stir together the oil, sage, and thyme in a small bowl to make a wet paste. Cut several shallow slashes in the skin side of the pork belly so that the fat will cook out. Rub the paste over the meat and season with a generous amount of salt and pepper. Take a big sauté pan and put it over medium-high heat. Add a 2-count of olive oil and get the oil smoking hot. Add the pork, skin side down, and cook for 4 to 5 minutes, until it's nice and brown. Turn the pork over and remove the pan from the heat. Carefully drain the fat from the pan. Add the cider and stock and cover the whole thing with foil or a lid. Put it in the oven and braise for about 1 hour or a little longer, until the meat is very tender.

While that's working, get going on the apples. Core the apples with an apple corer, making a good-size cavity to hold the stuffing. In a mixing bowl, combine the softened butter, muffin crumbs, raisins, sage, garlic, 3 tablespoons of the brown sugar, salt, and pepper. Spoon the stuffing into the cavities of the cored apples and stand them up, side by side, in a baking dish. Sprinkle the tops with the remaining tablespoon of brown sugar.

When the pork has cooked for 30 minutes, pour the cup of cider around the apples and bake for 30 to 35 minutes, until soft when pierced with a knife.

When the pork is cooked, take the pan out of the oven and put it over medium-high heat. Bring to a boil, reduce the heat, and simmer, basting the pork with the juices, until the juices are reduced and thickened to a saucelike consistency. Remove the pork to a cutting board and cut it into slices. Taste the sauce and check for seasoning; add a little lemon juice if the sauce needs brightening. Arrange on a platter with the baked apples and serve with the cider gravy along with Mashed Potatoes and Celery Root (page 250).

NOTE | You can also make this recipe with a 4- to 5-pound pork shoulder; braise for about 3 hours, until the internal temperature registers 150°F. to 160°F.

¹/₂ cup extra-virgin olive oil

Leaves from a small bunch of fresh sage, chopped

Leaves from a small bunch of fresh thyme, chopped

1 slice (about 2 pounds) fresh unsmoked pork belly (see Note)

Kosher salt and freshly ground black pepper

2 (12-ounce) bottles hard or sweet cider

2 cups chicken stock, homemade (see page 36) or store-bought

BUTTERED APPLES

8 apples, such as Gala

¹/₄ cup (¹/₂ stick) unsalted butter, softened to room temperature

1 large corn muffin, crumbled (¹/₂ cup of crumbs)

¹/₂ cup golden raisins

6 fresh sage leaves, chopped

2 garlic cloves, minced

4 tablespoons dark brown sugar

Kosher salt and freshly ground black pepper

1 cup hard or sweet cider

1 tablespoon fresh lemon juice, if needed

Mashed Potatoes and Celery Root

45 minutes | Serves 8

Potatoes are fantastic on their own, mashed with butter and cream, but paired up with celery root, the purée has a sweet, earthy root flavor.

2 celery root (celeriac) bulbs (about 3 pounds total), peeled and cut into 1-inch cubes | 3 pounds baking potatoes, peeled and cut into 1-inch cubes | Kosher salt and freshly ground black pepper | $^1/_2$ cup heavy cream | $^1/_2$ cup (1 stick) unsalted butter | Chopped fresh chives, for garnish | Extra-virgin olive oil

Put the celery root and potatoes in a medium saucepan with cold water to cover. Add 1 teaspoon salt, bring to a boil, reduce the heat, and simmer for 15 to 20 minutes, until the vegetables are very tender. Drain, reserving $^1/_2$ cup of the cooking liquid. Pass the vegetables through a food mill or a ricer into a large mixing bowl. Stir in the cream and butter until the cream is absorbed and the mixture is smooth. Add enough of the reserved cooking liquid to make a very soft purée. Season with salt and pepper and garnish with chopped chives and a drizzle of olive oil.

Braised Brisket

45 minutes + about 3 hours to braise | Serves 10

I like to serve the vegetables and brisket in separate bowls because they look really beautiful that way. But if you like, you can just throw the potatoes in with the brisket about 30 minutes before it's done, cook the cabbage in that same pot for a few minutes right at the end, and serve the whole thing together.

BRISKET

4 large garlic cloves, peeled and smashed

Kosher salt

Needles from 4 sprigs of fresh rosemary, chopped

Extra-virgin olive oil

1 (4-pound) first-cut beef brisket

Preheat the oven to 325°F.

On a cutting board, mash the garlic and $^1/_2$ teaspoon of salt to a paste with the flat side of a knife. Add the rosemary and mash that in, too. Put the garlic–rosemary paste in a small bowl and add 2 tablespoons of olive oil. Stir to combine.

Season both sides of the brisket with a fair amount of kosher salt and ground pepper. Put a large roasting pan or Dutch oven over medium-high heat and coat with a 2-count of olive oil. Put the brisket in the roasting pan and sear to form a nice brown crust on both sides. Lay the vegetables all around the brisket and drizzle the garlic–rosemary paste over the whole thing. Add the wine and tomatoes. Toss in the parsley and bay leaves. Cover the pan tightly with aluminum foil or a lid and put it in the oven. Cook for about 3 hours, basting every 30 minutes with the pan juices, until the beef is tender enough to cut with a fork.

About 30 minutes before the brisket is cooked, put the potatoes in a large pot and add cold, salted water to cover. Bring to a boil, reduce the heat, and simmer until the potatoes are tender. In a small bowl, stir together the butter, herbs, minced garlic, and salt and pepper to taste.

Remove the brisket to a cutting board and let it rest for 15 minutes. Scoop the vegetables out of the roasting pan and onto a platter, and cover to keep warm. Spoon off most of the fat, and put the roasting pan with the pan juices over medium-high heat. Boil, stirring and scraping to pick up any bits on the bottom, for 5 minutes, or until the sauce is reduced by about half. (If you want a thicker sauce, stir together the flour and 2 tablespoons of wine or water and whisk that into the gravy.)

While you've got the sauce and potatoes going, cook the cabbage. Bring the chicken stock to a boil in a large saucepan. Add the half head of garlic and the cabbage leaves and simmer until the cabbage is just tender, 2 to 3 minutes. Remove the cabbage from the broth with a basket strainer or slotted spoon and put it into a serving bowl. Pour in enough of the stock to moisten. Drain the potatoes and toss them in another serving bowl with the herb butter to coat.

To serve, slice the brisket across the grain (the muscle lines) at a slight diagonal; put the meat on the platter with the roasted vegetables and spoon the sauce over. Serve with the potatoes and cabbage.

Coarsely ground black pepper

4 large carrots, peeled and cut into 3-inch lengths

3 celery stalks, cut into 3-inch lengths

4 large red onions, halved

2 cups dry red wine, plus extra if needed

1 (14-ounce) can whole tomatoes, hand crushed

1 handful of fresh flat-leaf parsley

3 bay leaves

1 tablespoon all-purpose flour (optional)

NEW POTATOES

3 pounds new potatoes

Kosher salt and freshly ground black pepper

$^1/4$ cup ($^1/2$ stick) unsalted butter, at room temperature

2 tablespoons chopped fresh flat-leaf parsley

2 teaspoons fresh thyme leaves

1 garlic clove, minced

CABBAGE

1 quart chicken stock, homemade (see page 36) or store-bought

$^1/2$ head of garlic

1 large head of Savoy cabbage, quartered, cored, and leaves separated

LICKING THE PLATE CLEAN

MY FAVORITE DESSERTS are the ones that don't take five hours to create. The old restaurant philosophy of elaborate preparations and garnishes is completely thrown out the window in this chapter. **IT'S ALL ABOUT THE FLAVOR AND TASTE.** I like desserts that are thought-provoking and actually taste good.

LICKING
THE PLATE
CLEAN

Greek Yogurt with a Fig, Date, and Honey Swirl

20 minutes | Serves 4

Try to get the best-quality yogurt you can find for this; Greek yogurt is usually best because it's so dense and super-creamy. And swirled with the warm honey-dried fruit sauce, this packs an incredible flavor combination in one spoon.

Put the figs, dates, honey, water, lemon juice, and cinnamon stick in a small saucepan over medium heat. Simmer, partially covered, for about 10 minutes, until the fruit is soft. Set that aside and let it cool slightly. Discard the cinnamon stick.

Meanwhile, toast the nuts in a sauté pan over medium heat for 3 to 5 minutes, until fragrant. Transfer to a plate to cool, then roughly chop.

To serve, spoon about ½ cup yogurt onto a dessert plate or bowl and spoon some of the warm fruit over it. Sprinkle with nuts and garnish with mint leaves. Plate up 3 more desserts the same way and serve immediately.

NOTE | Greek yogurt is thicker and less sour than plain yogurt.

6 figs, fresh or dried, quartered
6 dates, pitted
¹/₂ cup honey
¹/₄ cup water
Juice of 1 lemon
1 cinnamon stick
¹/₄ cup chopped walnuts
¹/₄ cup chopped almonds
¹/₄ cup pine nuts
2 cups plain yogurt, preferably Greek (see Note)
Fresh mint leaves, for garnish

Pistachio Meringues with Warm Strawberries

1 hour | Serves 6

I think meringues are really overlooked in America, as a dessert. These are cloudlike in the center—like a marshmallow. The outside is crisp and brittle and the pistachios give them a great, nutty flavor.

4 large egg whites

1 cup plus 2 tablespoons sugar

1 teaspoon pure vanilla extract

$1/2$ cup finely chopped (but not powdered) pistachios

1 pint strawberries, hulled and cut into thick slices

Juice of $1/2$ lemon

Start by putting your whites in the bowl of an electric mixer so they're set to go. Then make your sugar syrup: Bring 1 cup of water to a low boil, add the cup of sugar, and cook to dissolve. Then bring the syrup to a boil and cook until the syrup reaches 248°F. on a candy thermometer. When the syrup is almost up to temperature, beat the egg whites to stiff peaks. Then, with the mixer going, gradually pour in the hot sugar syrup and keep beating until cool. Beat in the vanilla.

Preheat the oven to 275°F. Line a baking sheet with parchment paper. Using two large spoons, first scoop out a big spoonful of the meringue mixture. Then use the other spoon to push the meringue off onto the parchment-lined baking sheet so that you have a big free-form mountain peak of meringue. Keep going this same way to use all of the meringue. Sprinkle with the pistachios. Put the baking sheet in the oven and bake for 30 to 40 minutes, until the outsides of the meringues are set and crisp and the insides are still soft like marshmallows. Remove from the oven and transfer to wire racks to cool.

When the meringues are out of the oven, get your strawberries on. Combine the strawberries, the remaining 2 tablespoons of sugar, and the lemon juice in a nonreactive saucepan and warm over medium heat just until the strawberries begin to break down and give off their juices, about 3 minutes. Serve the meringues with the warm strawberries and their juices.

Muscat Gelée with Blackberries and Rosemary

45 minutes + chilling | Serves 4

Wine jellies in the summer make a perfect, impressive dessert. They're really easy to throw together and are a good way to introduce yourself to Muscat, one of the greatest dessert wines on the planet. This looks really pretty in martini glasses, too.

Put the blackberries in a bowl and sprinkle with 1 tablespoon of the sugar. Twist the rosemary in your hands to crush the needles a bit—that releases the essential oils—and throw it on top. Gently toss the berries to get them coated with the sugar and let them sit, absorbing the flavor of the rosemary, while you make the gelée.

Combine half of the bottle of Muscat (put the rest of the bottle in the fridge to serve with the dessert), the lemon juice, orange zest, and the remaining 2 tablespoons of sugar in a heavy saucepan and put it over medium-low heat. Simmer and stir until little bubbles appear on the surface and the alcohol starts to vaporize, about 15 minutes.

While that's cooking, soak the gelatin sheets in cool water for 2 minutes to soften (or, if using powdered gelatin, combine with 2 tablespoons cool water and let stand for 3 minutes). Take the wine off the heat and fish out the strips of orange zest. Take the gelatin sheets out of the water, squeeze to remove the excess, and add to the hot wine (or just pour the powdered gelatin mixture into the wine). Put the wine back on the heat and continue to simmer for 1 more minute, stirring to completely dissolve the gelatin. Take the pan off the heat and let the gelée cool for 5 minutes.

Fill 4 glasses one-quarter full with blackberries. Carefully pour the gelée over the berries to fill the glasses to the top. Chill until thoroughly gelled and set, at least 4 hours or up to overnight. Garnish the gelée with whipped cream, mint, and rosemary and serve with the remaining half-bottle of Muscat.

2 pints fresh blackberries, halved

3 tablespoons sugar

2 fresh rosemary sprigs, plus more for garnish

1 (750-ml) bottle Muscat or other sweet dessert wine

Juice of $^1/_2$ lemon

2 large strips of orange zest

2 gelatin sheets or 1 envelope (2$^1/_4$ teaspoons) powdered gelatin

Sweetened whipped cream, for serving

Fresh mint leaves, for garnish

Peach and Blueberry Crostata

1 $1/2$ hours | Serves 6 to 8

I named this dish (aka The Sepulveda Tart) for a really good friend in Los Angeles who could never remember how to make it. You don't need a tart pan and the only thing you need to focus on is the quality of the crust and the ingredients. The simple, rustic presentation is a real conversation piece.

PASTRY DOUGH

2 cups all-purpose flour, plus more
for rolling

3 tablespoons sugar

$1/4$ teaspoon salt

Zest of 1 lemon, finely grated

$3/4$ cup (1 $1/2$ sticks) cold, unsalted
butter, cut into small chunks

1 large egg yolk

2 tablespoons ice water, plus more
if needed

FILLING

4 large ripe peaches

1 pint fresh blueberries

Juice of $1/2$ lemon

2 tablespoons sugar

2 teaspoons all-purpose flour

1 large egg, beaten with a drizzle
of cold water

2 tablespoons sugar

Vanilla ice cream, for serving

Combine the flour, sugar, salt, and lemon zest in a large mixing bowl. Add the butter and mix with a pastry blender or your fingers until the mixture resembles coarse crumbs. Add the egg yolk and the ice water and work that in with your hands. (Or do the whole thing in the food processor, pulsing a couple of times to combine the dry ingredients, pulsing in the butter, and then the egg and water.) You want there to be just enough moisture to bind the dough so that it holds together without being too wet or sticky, so check the consistency: squeeze a small amount of the dough together between your thumb and forefingers. If it's still crumbly, add a little more ice water, 1 teaspoon at a time. When you get it to the right consistency, shape the dough into a disk and wrap it in plastic. Put it in the refrigerator and chill for at least 30 minutes.

When the dough has chilled, preheat the oven to 450°F. Put a pizza stone in the oven to heat, if you have one.

Cut the peaches in half, discard the pits, slice in a large bowl. Add the blueberries, lemon juice, sugar, and flour and toss to coat; set aside.

Sprinkle the counter and a rolling pin lightly with flour. Roll the dough out to a 14-inch round, about $1/4$ inch thick. It doesn't have to be a perfect circle; free form is good. Transfer the dough to a lightly floured pizza paddle. (If you don't have a pizza stone and paddle, transfer to the back of a jelly-roll pan; you'll put that right in the oven.) Spoon the filling mixture over the center of the dough round, leaving a 2-inch border all around. Brush the border with the egg wash. Bring the edge of crust over onto the filling, leaving the fruit exposed in the center. Gently fold and pinch the dough to seal any cracks. Brush the crust with the remaining egg wash and sprinkle with the sugar. Transfer to the pizza stone (or put the pan in the oven) and bake for 30 minutes, or until the crust is golden brown and the fruit is bubbly and tender. Slide a knife under the tart to loosen it from the stone or pan. Then cut into wedges and serve warm or at room temperature with vanilla ice cream.

Warm Blueberry Madeleines with Lemon Curd

1 hour + at least 2 hours chilling time | Serves 6 to 8

Warm blueberry madeleines dipped in creamy lemon curd make a great interactive dessert. I'll put a big platter of madeleines on the table and it's a free-for-all until you get to the very last, lonely one. Everyone sits there for a while, staring at it . . . staring at each other . . . trying to be polite, but it's just not possible. I always end up making more.

To make the lemon curd, bring about 2 inches of water to a simmer in a medium saucepan or double boiler over medium-low heat. Combine the egg yolks, sugar, and lemon juice and zest in a metal or heat-resistant glass bowl or in the top of a double boiler and whisk until smooth. Set the bowl over—not in—the simmering water (the bottom should not touch the water) and keep whisking. Keep working out that arm, whisking the curd vigorously for a good 10 minutes, until it has doubled in volume and is very thick and yellow. Don't let it boil. Remove the bowl from the heat and whisk in the butter, a couple of chunks at a time, until incorporated. Refrigerate until the curd is cold and firm.

You can start right away on the madeleines. Sift the flour with the baking powder into a mixing bowl. In another bowl, whisk the sugar and the eggs together until well mixed. Whisk in the orange zest. Then fold in the flour mixture, sifting it over the egg mixture in three batches. When the last batch is almost incorporated, with just a little flour still visible, drizzle the butter over the batter and fold in very gently—you want to lose as little volume as possible. Stick that in the refrigerator until the butter begins to harden, 20 to 30 minutes.

Preheat the oven to 400°F. Butter and flour two madeleine molds. When the batter is cold, spoon it into the molds, filling each about two-thirds full. Dot the top of each with 4 or 5 blueberries, pressing them gently into the batter. Bake until golden brown, 12 to 15 minutes. Let the madeleines cool for a few minutes on a wire rack, then remove. Serve these babies warm, dipping them into the curd.

LEMON CURD

6 large egg yolks

1 cup sugar

Juice and zest of 4 lemons

¹/₂ cup (1 stick) unsalted butter, cut into chunks

MADELEINES

1 cup all-purpose flour

1 teaspoon baking powder

²/₃ cup sugar

4 large eggs

Grated zest of 1 orange

¹/₂ cup (1 stick) unsalted butter, melted and cooled, pus more for greasing the molds

¹/₂ pint fresh blueberries

Yellow Butter Cake with Red Fruits

1 ¹/₂ hours + at least 1 hour to cool the cake | Serves 8 to 10

I've made this recipe a hundred times and every time it has a huge wow factor. It's easy to make with just one sheet pan.

BUTTER CAKE

2 ¹/₂ cups cake flour

2 teaspoons baking powder

¹/₂ teaspoon salt

³/₄ cup (1 ¹/₂ sticks) unsalted butter, at room temperature

1 ³/₄ cups sugar

6 large eggs, separated

1 teaspoon pure vanilla extract

1 ¹/₂ cups milk

ICING

3 large egg whites

2 ¹/₄ cups sugar

¹/₃ cup cold water

1 ¹/₂ tablespoons light corn syrup

RED FRUITS

Juice of ¹/₂ lemon

¹/₄ cup Grand Marnier

¹/₄ cup sugar

1 vanilla bean, split and scraped

1 pint strawberries, hulled and halved

¹/₂ pint raspberries

¹/₂ pint cherries

¹/₂ pint fresh currants

Grand Marnier, for soaking the cake

Preheat the oven to 325°F. Spray a 13 × 18-inch jelly-roll pan with non-stick spray, line it with parchment paper, and spray that, too.

Sift the flour with the baking powder and salt into a bowl; set aside. In the bowl of an electric mixer, cream the butter with the sugar until lightened. Add the egg yolks, one by one, beating well after each. Beat in the vanilla. Then beat in the dry ingredients in three batches, alternating with the milk, and beat until smooth. In another bowl, beat the egg whites to stiff peaks. Fold the whites into the batter and pour into the prepared pan. Smooth the top. Bake until a cake tester stuck into the center comes out clean, about 35 minutes.

To make the icing, bring about 2 inches of water to a simmer in a medium saucepan over medium-low heat. Combine all of the ingredients in a metal or heat-resistant glass bowl. Set the bowl over—not in—the simmering water (the bottom should not touch the water) and beat with an electric mixer to stiff peaks. This should take 4 to 7 minutes, depending on your mixer. Then remove from the heat and keep beating until the icing is thick enough to spread.

For the fruits, combine the lemon juice and Grand Marnier in a small saucepan over medium heat. Add the sugar and vanilla scrapings and cook, stirring constantly, until the sugar has dissolved. Toss in the fruits and stir to coat with the liquid. Then cook for 3 more minutes, until the fruits begin to burst. Remove from the heat and let cool.

Once everything has cooled, you're ready to assemble the cake. First thing to do now is to add about ¼ cup of the cooled red fruit to the icing and stir it once—just to swirl the color through—so that the icing looks streaky. Now use a long, serrated knife to trim the domed top of the cake; that's going to make it easier to ice. Cut the cake into thirds to give you 3 narrow 13 × 6-inch rectangles. Put one cake rectangle on a cake stand and brush it with Grand Marnier. Slather with the icing and top with another cake rectangle. Brush with Grand Marnier and spread with some icing. Put the remaining cake rectangle on top, brush with Grand Marnier, and spread the top and the sides of the cake with the remaining icing. Pour the remaining fruit down the center of the cake.

Miles's Strawberry Soup

30 minutes | Serves 4

My sous-chef and recipe collaborator (my son) insisted that we have a fruit soup in this chapter. This recipe is very simple and it's really good.

Combine the strawberries, sugar, and lemon juice in a medium saucepan over medium heat. Cook, stirring every now and then, until the fruit cooks down and thickens to a compote, 15 to 20 minutes. Let that cool.

About 20 minutes before you're ready to serve, scoop the ice cream out into a bowl and let it sit at room temperature until it's a sort of soupy, slushy, half-frozen consistency. Swirl in the compote and serve.

1 pint strawberries, hulled and chopped
$1/4$ cup sugar
Juice of $1/2$ lemon
1 pint excellent-quality strawberry ice cream

Miles's Snowman Soup

15 minutes | Serves 4

My son, Miles, and I were sitting in a restaurant in Stowe, Vermont, a few Christmases ago when the waitress came by and asked us what we wanted to drink. Miles said he wanted "snowman soup." We laughed and I couldn't figure out what he was talking about. So I asked him to describe it and what he was describing was hot chocolate. I thought the name was hysterical. So he and I collaborated and put this recipe together. He said it should taste like "a melted chocolate snowman."

Heat the milk nearly to a boil (scalding) and take it off the heat. Add the sugar and chocolate and stir until melted. Spoon 2 tablespoons of cocoa powder into each of 4 large mugs. Pour in the chocolate milk and stir. Top with marshmallows and sprinkles.

1 quart milk
$3/4$ cup sugar
8 ounces excellent-quality bittersweet chocolate (70%), chopped
$1/2$ cup cocoa powder
20 medium-size marshmallows
Sprinkles, for serving

Clafoutis with Sauternes-Soaked Prunes

1 ¼ hours | Serves 6

When my dad came out to visit me in France last summer, he wanted to make something for dinner. So we flipped through a few old French cookbooks and came across a clafoutis, a dessert that is something like a cross between a muffin and a soufflé, but is baked in a large dish. My dad's a really good cook and it turned out great. With a little bit of cold vanilla ice cream, it's a stunner.

2 cups pitted prunes

¹/₂ lemon

1 cup Sauternes or other dessert wine

1 tablespoon plus ¹/₄ cup sugar, plus more for dusting the pie pan

³/₄ cup all-purpose flour

Pinch of salt

3 large eggs

1 ¹/₄ cups milk

1 teaspoon pure vanilla extract

¹/₃ cup slivered almonds

Put the prunes in a bowl, squeeze the lemon juice over them, pour in the Sauternes, and sprinkle with the tablespoon of sugar. Toss that and let it sit for 30 minutes so that the prunes soak up the flavor of the wine.

Preheat the oven to 325°F. Butter a 9-inch pie pan and dust it with sugar. In a mixing bowl, sift together the remaining ¼ cup sugar, the flour, and salt. Add the eggs, milk, and vanilla and beat until smooth. Take the prunes out of the wine with a slotted spoon and arrange them over the bottom of the prepared pan. Pour the batter over the fruit and smooth the top; sprinkle with the slivered almonds. Bake the clafoutis for 30 to 40 minutes, until risen and just firm. Serve warm.

Dark Chocolate Cake with Chocolate Mousse and Toasted Coconut

2 hours + at least 1 hour to cool | Serves 8 to 10

Whole, large, paper-thin rounds of coconut give this cake lots of character. And the mousse is surprisingly easy to pull off.

CHOCOLATE CAKE

3/4 cup (1 1/2 sticks) unsalted butter, at room temperature, plus more for greasing the pans

2 1/2 cups cake flour, plus more for dusting the pans

2 teaspoons baking powder

1/2 teaspoon salt

1 3/4 cups sugar

8 ounces bittersweet chocolate (70%), melted

6 large eggs, separated

1 teaspoon pure vanilla extract

1 1/2 cups milk

RUM SYRUP

2 cups sugar

1/4 cup spiced dark rum

CHOCOLATE MOUSSE

8 ounces bittersweet chocolate (70%), chopped

3 tablespoons unsalted butter

4 large eggs, separated

1 cup heavy cream

1/2 pound fresh coconut, sliced into paper-thin rings and toasted

Start with the cake. Preheat the oven to 325°F. Butter and flour two 9-inch cake pans. Sift the flour with the baking powder and salt into a bowl; set aside. In the bowl of an electric mixer, cream the butter with the sugar until lightened. Beat in the melted chocolate. Then add the egg yolks, one by one, beating well after each. Beat in the vanilla. Then beat in the dry ingredients in three batches, alternating with the milk, and beat until smooth.

In another bowl, beat the egg whites to stiff peaks, then fold into the batter. Pour the batter into the prepared pans and smooth the tops. Bake until a cake tester stuck into the centers comes out clean, about 35 minutes. Let cool for 3 minutes in the pans on a rack. Then invert the pans to unmold, and cool the layers completely on the rack.

While the cake bakes and cools, make the rum syrup. You'll brush this on the cake layers to add flavor and moistness. Bring 2 cups of water to a low boil over medium heat in a saucepan. Stir in the sugar and cook until dissolved, about 1 minute. Stir in the rum and set aside to cool.

Now turn to the mousse. Bring about 2 inches of water to a simmer in a medium saucepan or double boiler over medium-low heat. Combine the chocolate and butter in a metal or heat-resistant glass bowl or in the top of a double boiler and set over—not in—the simmering water (the bottom should not touch the water). Cook until the chocolate is just melted; stir until smooth. Take the mixture off the heat and stir in the egg yolks while the chocolate is still warm (the heat will poach the yolks). Scrape that out into a bowl and let cool. In another bowl, beat the cream to soft peaks, then fold it carefully into the cooled chocolate mixture. Beat the egg whites to stiff peaks in a clean bowl and fold them in, too. Finally, measure out about 1/2 cup of the toasted coconut (save the rest for garnish) and gently fold that in.

Now it's time to put it all together. With a long, serrated knife, trim off the rounded top of each cooled cake layer to level them. Then slice each cake layer in half horizontally so that you have four thin layers. Put one layer on a cake stand and brush with the rum syrup. Slather the cake with about one quarter of the mousse. Sprinkle with some of the reserved toasted coconut. Put another cake layer on top and press down lightly—some of the frosting should squeeze out the sides (like a cartoon cake). Brush with the syrup, spread with more mousse, and sprinkle with coconut. Repeat the process twice more to use all of the cake and mousse, making sure that the mousse between the layers shows on the side of the cake. Sprinkle the top generously with the remaining coconut but do not ice the sides of the cake.

Warm and Crusty Date Pudding

45 minutes | Serves 8

Dates and chocolate—the new Bernie Taupin and Elton John.

Preheat the oven to 375°F. and move an oven rack to the middle of the oven. Spray a 1½-quart soufflé dish with nonstick spray.

Put the dates into a saucepan and add ¾ cup of water. Bring to a simmer and cook over medium-low heat for 10 minutes, or until the dates are very soft and the water is mostly evaporated. Transfer to a food processor and purée until smooth. Add the sugar and vanilla and process until well blended. Scrape out into a large mixing bowl.

Now rinse out the saucepan and put the cream into it. Bring the cream to a simmer, take the pan off the heat, and stir in the chocolate until melted. Pour that into the bowl with the date mixture and stir until smooth. In another bowl, sift together the cocoa powder and flour and fold into the chocolate–date mixture with a rubber spatula until well mixed. In a separate bowl, whip the egg whites until they form stiff peaks. Fold that into the date mixture and your batter's done. Pour it into the prepared dish and smooth the top with a spatula. Bake on the middle rack for 25 minutes, or until the outside of the pudding is set and crusty looking. Let cool until the pudding is just warm. Then sift confectioners' sugar all over the top.

2 cups pitted dates (6 ounces)

1 ¼ cups sugar

1 tablespoon pure vanilla extract

¼ cup heavy cream

4 ounces semisweet chocolate, chopped into pieces

½ cup unsweetened cocoa powder

¼ cup all-purpose flour

6 large egg whites

Confectioners' sugar, for garnish

Lemon Ginger Ice

30 minutes + 1 to 2 hours to chill the syrup | Serves 8

This is one of my favorite dessert recipes. It takes no time to put together because the "slushy" is made in the blender. It has the smooth flavor of a sorbet and the ginger syrup is very understated; it tastes like a frozen lemonade.

8 medium to large lemons

2 egg whites, lightly beaten

1 ½ cups sugar, plus more for coating the lemon "cups"

2-inch piece of fresh ginger, peeled and sliced

Zest of 1 lemon, finely grated

Crushed ice

Fresh mint leaves, for garnish

To make the lemon cups: Trim a very thin slice off of the bottom of each lemon so they'll be stable when you stand them up. Cut off the top quarter of each lemon and reserve these as caps for the cups. Carefully hollow out the lemons with a teaspoon, leaving the shells intact. Reserve the pulp and juice. Paint the outsides of the shells and caps with egg white and roll in granulated sugar to coat. Now take an empty egg carton and set the lemon shells and caps in there. Freeze for at least 1 hour or up to overnight. The frozen shell will keep the lemon ice from melting too quickly when you serve.

Combine the 1½ cups of sugar, 2 cups of water, and the ginger slices in a pot over medium heat. Gently simmer and stir for 2 minutes, or until the sugar is dissolved and the ginger fragrant; do not allow the syrup to boil or get dark. Remove from the heat, cover, put it in the refrigerator, and let steep until cold.

Pass the reserved lemon juice and pulp through a sieve into a blender. When the syrup is cold, fish out the pieces of ginger and pour the syrup into the blender. Add the lemon zest. Then add crushed ice and process until slushy. Spoon the slush into the frozen lemon cups, top each with a cap, garnish with mint leaves, and serve.

Basil Ice Cream with Wine-Poached Cherries

30 minutes + 2 hours to chill | Serves 6

Last summer in France we cooked dinner every night, and every night we cooked, we made dessert. This was our hands-down favorite. It's a freezer-box ice cream made with heavy cream, crème fraîche, and fresh basil leaves. It has a sweet, herby flavor, and paired up with the red-wine syrup and sweet cherries, it tastes like a warm summer night in Provence.

Combine the heavy cream, crème fraîche, lemon zest, and vanilla scrapings in a saucepan. Bring to a simmer and remove from the heat. In a heat-proof mixing bowl, whisk the egg yolks with the sugar until lightened. Throw in a handful of the basil leaves. Then pour in the hot cream mixture and stir for 5 minutes just to get the flavor of the basil into the cream. Strain into a bowl and cool in an ice bath. When the cream is nice and cold, throw in the rest of the basil and let that sit until you're ready to freeze, or 5 to 10 minutes. Pour into a baking dish, cover, and put the ice cream in the freezer.

Now turn your attention to the cherries. Combine the cherries, sugar, wine, vanilla scrapings, and lemon in a saucepan. Bring to a simmer and cook over medium-high heat for 10 to 15 minutes, until the cherries are softened and the liquid has reduced a little around them. Take the pan off the heat and set it aside until you're ready to serve.

After about 2 hours, the ice cream will have just started to set but it will still be soft; this is the time to eat it. Take a big spoon and chunk out big fat pieces of the semi-frozen ice cream. Rewarm the cherries, and serve them with the ice cream.

BASIL ICE CREAM

1 quart heavy cream

1 cup crème fraîche

1 strip of lemon zest

$^1/_2$ vanilla bean, split and scraped

4 large egg yolks

$^1/_2$ cup sugar

2 big handfuls of fresh basil leaves, torn into pieces

CHERRIES

1 pound fresh cherries, pitted

2 tablespoons sugar

1 $^1/_2$ cups red wine

1 vanilla bean, split and scraped

Juice of $^1/_2$ lemon

WHEN YOU BITE INTO A BOSC PEAR,
YOU REALLY KNOW WHAT TIME OF YEAR IT IS.

Warm Pear Tart with Blue Cheese and Honey

1 hour | Serves 6 to 8

This recipe tastes delicious in the same way that peanut brittle tastes delicious: The pear and the honey are sweet and the blue cheese is salty.

1 sheet of frozen puff pastry cut in half lengthwise to make 2 long rectangles

1 pound blanched almonds

¼ cup sugar

6 pears (use 3 different varieties, with different shapes and colors), stemmed and sliced (seeds, skins, and all)

Honey

4 ounces good-quality blue cheese

1 egg white beaten with a drizzle of water, for glazing

Preheat the oven to 400°F. Lay one of the pastry rectangles on the back of a sheet pan; save the other rectangle for another use. Use a paring knife to score a line around the perimeter of the rectangle, about 1 inch from the edge, to make a border. Use a fork to poke holes inside the border so that the dough will remain flat as it cooks; the border will puff to create a lip for the tart.

Combine the almonds, sugar, and 1 tablespoon of water in a food processor and grind to a paste. Spread the paste over just the inside of the pastry rectangle. Arrange the pear slices over the almond paste. Drizzle with honey and crumble the blue cheese over the top.

Brush the pastry border with egg glaze and bake until the pastry is puffed and browned, 25 to 30 minutes.

Chocolate Tart

1 1/2 hours + at least 30 minutes to chill the dough I Serves 6 to 8

This is one for the in-laws if they ever come to town. The crust has a nice snap to it and the chocolate is very creamy.

Roll out the dough on a lightly floured surface to a 12-inch circle, about 1/4 inch thick. Carefully roll the dough up onto the pin (this may take a little practice) and lay it inside a 9-inch tart pan with a removable bottom. Gently press the dough into the pan; it is important to fit the dough evenly into every nook and cranny of the pan, especially the scalloped edges. Shave off the excess dough with a knife.

Preheat the oven to 350°F. Put the tart shell on a sturdy baking sheet so it will be easy to move in and out of the oven. Line the shell with aluminum foil and add pie weights or dried beans to keep the sides of the tart from buckling. Put that in the oven and bake for 30 minutes. Then take the tart out of the oven and remove the foil along with the weights or beans. Using a pastry brush, lightly coat the shell all over with a thin layer of egg white. Return to the oven and continue to bake until the shell is cooked through and a light golden color, but not browned, about 8 minutes. (The tart will be cooked again with the filling; you don't want it to burn on the second bake.) Set aside to cool while you make the filling. Turn the oven down to 325°F.

To make the filling, combine the heavy cream and milk in a saucepan and heat it over medium-low until the mixture just simmers slightly around the edges. Take the pan off the heat, add the chopped chocolate, and stir until it's good and smooth. Add the sugar and salt and whisk until well incorporated. Let sit for 5 minutes to cool slightly. Then beat the eggs in a small bowl until blended. Stir them into the chocolate mixture and whisk until it's all completely blended. Pour the filling into the cooled tart shell and bake for 15 to 20 minutes, until the filling is set and the surface is glossy. If you see any bubbles or cracks forming on the surface, take the tart out right away—that means it is beginning to overcook. Cool before cutting and serve warm.

1 recipe pastry dough (see page 260), wrapped and chilled for 30 minutes
All-purpose flour, for rolling
1 egg white, lightly beaten

FILLING
1 cup heavy cream
1/2 cup milk
8 ounces excellent-quality bittersweet chocolate (70%), chopped
1/4 cup sugar
1/4 teaspoon salt
2 large eggs, at room temperature

ACKNOWLEDGMENTS>>

After my second go at it, I think I have finally found the trick of putting together a cookbook. Surround yourself with the most talented people you can find, throw the idea of the project at them and pray they don't quit. Making a cookbook isn't easy and this project was no exception. *Eat This Book* took a year and a half to write, test, shoot, rewrite, and then edit, and I want to say how proud I am of it and the great energy that everyone put into the project, starting with Eileen Connors, my associate at Food Works Productions—not just for the collaboration, planning, and late-night conference calls, but for life in general. She makes the impossible seem doable with endless amounts of patience and grace. The book was co-penned with the brilliant food writer Stephiane Lyness, who really bent over backward to be available with my impossible schedule. It's the first of many, Steph, thanks.

If you've already flipped through this book and were blown away by the photographs, you're not alone. The first time I saw the photos that Petrina Tinslay had taken of my food, my jaw dropped. I'm lucky that our paths crossed and I truly believe that you haven't seen food until it's been through the eyes of this amazingly inspired photographer. Petrina, thanks for the vision and sorry about the long flights from Sydney.

And I'd like to give a special thanks to my editor at Clarkson Potter, Pam Krauss, who truly turned on the lights in my life and for whom I have a profound respect. You're the best.

And speaking of talented people, that's just where the list starts. In random order, here's the crew: Thanks to: Amy McCafferty, Petrina's photo assistant. Alison Attenborough, Colin Flynn, and Jamie Kimm, food stylists to the stars, for the focus during the shoots. You guys are the best. "Crazy" Abby Jenkins for the props, plates, and two years of laughing my ass off on *Food 911,* you're the coolest. Kersti Bowser, aka "The Gourmet Butterfly" for testing the recipes and being by my side for the best two years of my life; the question is How was your weekend? David Domedion for polishing a lot of the recipes and all your professionalism on *Food 911,* you da man. JoAnn Cianculli, the west coast arm of Food Works, for a lot of early development of recipes in this book and for your dedication to one of the most rewarding friendships. I miss you, Jo Jo. John, Cheryl, Craig, Audrey, Amanda, Rachie, Annie, Tim the Pie Man, Kevin, Pete the Pimp, Bernie Beans, and everybody at Stone House Productions for two amazing years of shooting *Food 911.* Jennifer DeFilippi, Chris Pavone, and everyone at Clarkson Potter for keeping the show going. My food network family:

Brook Johnson, Jeanne Shanahan, Bob Tushman, and Mark Dissen. Tom Lekometros and Tim Wynter-Stoner of the Lawrence Group for building the dream kitchen. The Union Square Greenmarket, Florence Prime Meat Market, Murray's Cheese Shop, the Fulton Fish Market, the place on Long Island with the micro greens, Ottomanelli Brothers meat market, Petrossian Caviar, Cornell Cooperative Extension of Suffolk, NY, Marine Programs Division, Sang Lee Farms, Inc., Peconic, NY, owned by Fred and Karen Lee, Kim Tetrault and S.P.A.T. on the north fork of Long Island. Evyn Block, Max MacKenzie, Frankie DeCarlo, Andrei Petrov, Lauren Bergman, Maxine Ganer, Patrick Davis, Richard Eisenberg, Phillip Baltz, Becca Parris, Tammy Walker, Todd English, Tom Nally, Michael Barrett, Kevin Berg, and Larry Silver. And last but not least my family: Miles, Mom and John, Dad and Jan, Ryan, Warren the Worminator, Kristi, Alycia.

I would like to give special thanks to Poggenpohl, Sub-Zero-Wolf for the unbelievable kitchen. You can reach them at: www.poggenpohl-usa.com or by mail at: 145 US Highway 46W, Suite 200 Wayne, NJ 07470 www.subzero.com or by mail at: Sub-ZeroFreezer Company, P.O. Box 44130, Madison, WI 53744-4130, phone: 800.222.7820; Wolf Appliance Company, LLC, P.O. Box 44848, Madison, WI 53744, phone: 800.332.9513; Miele Inc., 9 Independence Way, Princeton, NJ 08540, www.miele.com

Note: *Italicized* page numbers
refer to photographs.

LATER>>